THE GREAT CABLE CAR
ADVENTURE BOOK

My best wishes.

Gene Anthony

THE BALLAD OF
THE HYDE STREET GRIP

by Gelett Burgess

Oh, the rain is slanting sharply, and the Norther's blowing cold:
When the cable's strands are loosened she is nasty hard to
hold!
There's little time for sitting down, and little chance for gab,
For the bumper guards the crossing, and you'd best be keeping tab,
Two-and-twenty "let-go's" every double trip
It takes a lot of doing, on the Hyde Street Grip!

Throw her off at Powell Street, let her go at Post,
Watch her well at Geary and at Sutter when you coast!
Easy at the Power House, have a care at Clay,
Sacramento, Washington, Jackson—all the way!
Drop your rope at Union—never make a slip—
The lever keeps you busy, on the Hyde Street Grip!

Foot-brake, wheel-brake, slot-brake and gong,
You'd better keep 'em busy or you'll soon be going wrong!
Rush her on the crossing, catch her on the rise,
Easy round the corners when the dust is in your eyes—
And the bell will always stop you if you hit her up a clip;
You are apt to earn your wages on the Hyde Street Grip!

North Beach to Tenderloin, over Russian Hill,
The grades are something giddy, and the curves are fit to kill!
All the way to Market Street, clanging up the slope,
Down upon the other side, clinging to the rope!
But the view of San Francisco as you take the lurching dip!
There is plenty of excitement on the Hyde Street Grip!

If you had to drive a penny bus from Chelsea to the Strand
You'd see Westminster Abbey, and you'd say that it was grand!
If you had to pass the Luxembourg and Place de la Concorde
Atop a Paris omnibus, no doubt you'd thank the Lord!
But the Frenchy'd give his chapeau and the cockney give his whip
For a sight of San Francisco from the Hyde Street Grip!

Oh, the lights are in the Mission and the ships are on the Bay,
And Tamalpais is looming from the Gate, across the way;
The Presidio trees are waving, and the hills are growing brown,
And the driving fog is harried from the ocean to the town!
How the pulleys slap and rattle! How the cables hum and skip!
Oh, they sing a gallant chorus to the Hyde Street Grip!

When the Orpheum is closing and the crowds are on the way,
The conductor's punch is ringing and the dummy's light and gay;
But the wait upon the switch above the beach is dark and still —
Just the swashing of the surges on the shore below the Mill;
And the flash from Angel Island breaks across the Channel rip
As the hush of midnight falls upon the Hyde Street Grip!

(Published in A GAGE OF YOUTH — Boston: Small, Maynard and Company)

UP AND DOWN SAN FRANCISCO

THE
GREAT
CABLE CAR
ADVENTURE BOOK

A California Guide by
GENE ANTHONY AND JILL LOSSON

To all the cable car lovers of the world

Copyright © 1981 Gene Anthony and Jill Losson
Published by Presidio Press, Novato, California

Library of Congress Cataloging in Publication Data

Anthony, Gene.
  The great cable car adventure book.

  At head of title: Up and down San Francisco.
  Includes index.
    1. San Francisco (Calif.)——Description——Guide-
books. I. Losson, Jill, 1941–   II. Title.
F869.S33A57   917.94′610453   81-5919
ISBN 0-89141-120-8 (pbk.)   AACR2

ISBN 0-89141-120-8

Photographs by Gene Anthony
Designed by Jill Losson
Edited by Elaine Ratner and Tim Ware
Typesetting by Helen Epperson

Printed in the United States of America

CONTENTS

LIST OF MAPS

PREFACE

Why another guidebook to San Francisco? Frankly because, just like everyone else, we were enraptured by the sight of the cable cars hauling loads of beaming holiday visitors up and down the City's slopes. There is something magical about the cable cars; everyone seems to smile and open up when they ride them, even the natives. No matter what our mood, when we hop aboard, our spirits rise. We all become wide-eyed tourists again— until the conductor yells, "Last stop, everybody off."

A year ago a statistic caught our eye—95 percent of the visitors to San Francisco never ride any form of public transportation other than the cable cars. That figure gave life to this book. The Great Cable Car Adventure Book is for the 95 percent, because we found that 95 percent of the places most people want to visit are within easy walking distance of a cable car stop.

San Francisco, in spite of the hills, is a town made for walkers. Only on foot can you really experience the uniqueness of this sensuous city. Savor it step by step. Your eyes will meet an amazing variety of visual feasts, of architectural styles and vast panoramas. Your ears will encounter the sounds of whistles and bells, the humming of the cable through the slot of the cable car tracks, and the songs of birds nesting in the foliage and trees. More subtle is the aroma of roasting coffee in North Beach, the boiling crab pots on Fisherman's Wharf, or the fragrance of the eucalyptus, sage, and boxwood that line the stairways. So indulge yourself in this fabulous feast we call San Francisco. Grab your walking shoes and a warm jacket, and climb aboard.

ACKNOWLEDGMENTS

The research for this book was a marvelous experience and a rediscovery of our favorite city—San Francisco. We owe our appreciation and thanks to: Gladys Hansen, San Francisco Archivist; the California Historical Society; California Pioneers Society; the Bancroft Library; Joan Griffin and Bob Kane for their faith; Elaine Ratner and Tim Ware for their compassionate assistance; and Felix.

MAP OF CABLE CAR ROUTES

Cable car stops and tracks are indicated on this map as follows:

On the street they are indicated by bars marked across the tracks or MUNI signs posted on the sidewalk.

BEGINNING THE ADVENTURE

There is an excitement that prevails when vacation travelers first arrive in San Francisco. With so much in this city to see and do, where do you start? One of the first items on your list of things to do should be "ride a cable car." A round trip on one of the cable cars takes only about an hour. Then, knowing the lay of the land, you will be in a better position to pick out any one of dozens of exciting and interesting places to explore.

There are three cable car routes: the #59 Powell-Mason line, the #60 Powell-Hyde line and the #61 California line. For your first exploration, we suggest that you catch the Powell–Hyde Street cable car at the corner of Powell and Market streets. The views are spectacular, and the sounds and smells are an ever-changing delight. It leaves you off at the west end of the Fisherman's Wharf area. Then you can take a leisurely walk along the Wharf and return downtown on the Powell-Mason line. Our book follows this same route, covering the California Street line last. Following a capsule tour of these routes, together with the map at left, will help you get oriented.

Both the #59 Powell-Mason line and the #60 Powell-Hyde line begin at the Market Street turntable and travel up Powell Street with its many hotels, restaurants, and shops. After passing Union Square the cable cars begin the steep ascent to Nob Hill where they cross California Street, the location of

the City's third cable car line. They then proceed down the hill into an area bordering Chinatown, on the right. At Powell and Jackson streets the cable car track makes a left turn and runs for one block to Mason Street, the site of the Cable Car Barn and Museum. At this point the #59 and the #60 cable cars part company. The Powell-Hyde line continues up the hill to Hyde Street, turns right and follows the spine of Russian Hill, passing marvelous vistas of the City and the Bay. From the top of Russian Hill the cable car makes a breathtaking descent down Hyde Street to the end of the line at Aquatic Park. This is the west end of the Fisherman's Wharf area. Ghirardelli Square, the Maritime Museum, the Hyde Park Pier, and The Cannery are all within a block of this stop. When you depart the car you will see, due north, the Hyde Street Pier. Fisherman's Wharf begins there and continues east to Pier 39. West of the cable car turntable, on the border of the grassy area called Victorian Park, is the Maritime Museum. Across the street, on the hill above, sits Ghirardelli Square.

After you've explored the Museum and Ghirardelli Square, stroll three blocks east down Fisherman's Wharf to Taylor Street. Then turn right and walk three more blocks. You'll find enough in those six blocks to distract you for hours: The Cannery, The Anchorage, the fishing fleet tied up at the piers, the huge crab-cooking pots, shelves of San Francisco's famous sourdough bread, T-shirts, trinkets and, finally, Cost Plus, a huge import store. When you're done sightseeing, proceed up Taylor to Bay and you'll be at the end of the #59 Powell-Mason line. Most likely there will be a crowd waiting for the cable car.

The #59 cable car runs up Taylor to Columbus, skirting the Italian North Beach area, San Francisco's bohemia, and Broadway, the topless nightclub section. At Mason Street the cable car climbs the hill past the edge of Chinatown, on your left, and meets the #60 Powell-Hyde line near the Cable Car Barn and Museum. At this point the cable cars continue to Powell Street and on down to the Market Street turntable.

The #61 California line begins at Market and Drumm streets, adjacent to the Embarcadero Hyatt Regency Hotel. From Market Street the line travels through the City's financial district, then crosses Grant Avenue, the main Chinatown thoroughfare, then up to the top of Nob Hill. From the opulence of Nob Hill, the cable car descends to the Polk Gulch neighborhood and ends at Van Ness Avenue.

Cable car veterans usually manage to catch a ride regardless of how many passengers are jammed aboard. These riders rarely wait in line at the turntable, but catch the cars a few blocks away at the cable car street stops, which are indicated by either double white or yellow lines marked across the tracks or by brown and orange Muni signposts. The cable car's outside running board, closest to the middle of the street, always seems to have room for one or two more standing passengers. Two passengers are allowed between each of the four upright poles.

CABLE CAR SCHEDULE

The cable cars run 10 minutes apart throughout the daytime and evening hours. The schedule below gives you the departure times for the first and last car from each terminus.

#59 Powell-Mason Street Line:

Market Street Turntable	First car 6:33 A.M.	Last car 1:00 A.M.
Bay and Taylor Turntable	First car 6:14 A.M.	Last car 12:42 A.M.

#60 Powell-Hyde Street Line:

Market Street Turntable	First car 6:09 A.M.	Last car 12:51 A.M.
Beach and Hyde Turntable	First car 6:00 A.M.	Last car 12:30 A.M.

#61 California Street Line:

Drumm and Market Street	First car 6:22 A.M.	Last car 11:05 P.M.
Van Ness Avenue	First car 6:08 A.M.	Last car 10:45 P.M.

Schedules are subject to change and cable cars are subject to breakdowns. When the cable car system has to be stopped for repairs, MUNI operates buses along the routes.

For further information about cable cars or bus routes you can call 673-MUNI.

Ever since the first cable cars descended the steep slopes of a San Francisco hill over a century ago, they have captured the hearts and imagination of the whole world. Just the sight of the squat little cars rattling up and down the City's hills, swinging precariously around the curves with the gripman anxiously ringing the bell, is enough to lift the lowest of spirits.

It all began on a cool summer morning in 1873. The city newspaper of the time, the *Alta California*, recorded the great event, sandwiching it between news of a million-dollar fire in Oregon and an Indian war between the Sioux and the Pawnees in Wyoming.

Sunday, August 3, 1873—The first cable car ran down the Clay Street road yesterday. The street was lined with crowds of people anxious to see the workings of the dummies that aid in the propulsion of the cars. The car came down the hill from the upper end of the road and was hailed with delight by the multitudes that were stationed along the sidewalks. It made another trip up, but the ascent was slow as the machinery is yet new and consequently still stiff and awkward in its movement. However, the road may be written down as a success. These accomplishments have been long wished for in the community on the 'hill' and beyond.

"Hallidie's Folly" was one of several names that folks called Andrew Hallidie's little cable car enterprise during the 1870's. He was a wild-haired inventor who, with his father, had invented wire rope to help haul tons of gold and silver ore from the mines up in the gold country.

Thirty-five-year-old Andrew was inspired to invent the cable car after witnessing an accident. One wet night he was standing at a street corner watching horses struggling to pull crowded street cars up a steep incline. At one point a team of horses lost its footing and the street car started sliding, dragging its frantic passengers several hundred feet to the bottom of the hill. The event shocked Andrew and started him thinking about alternatives to this mode of transportation.

The first cable car track—2,800 feet—went down Clay Street. It started at Jones Street and ran down a 20-percent grade to Portsmouth Plaza, then the heart of downtown San Francisco. During the next sixteen years, seven new lines sprouted up and 110 miles of cable car track crisscrossed the City.

Today the cable cars are a national landmark managed by the San Francisco Municipal Railway, with ten miles of track and three separate lines.

The cable cars haven't really changed since those early days. Today's cars were built in Oakland, across the Bay, and first seen on our City's streets in 1887.

Basically, the cable cars are all built the same. The main body and frame are constructed of wood with some steel bracing. The Powell Street cars are single-ended; the California Street cars are double-ended with two complete sets of controls.

Control of the cable cars requires both a gripman and a conductor. The conductor, who is stationed in the rear of the car, collects the fares, operates the rear platform brake, and signals the gripman, who is in the front. Communication between the two, over the sounds of busy traffic and crowded cable cars, is accomplished by the ringing of a bell. Both a traffic bell and a communications bell are placed above the gripman's station; a third bell is located on the rear platform. One ring of the bell by the conductor means a passenger wants to get off at the next stop; two rings means proceed forward. A series of rings by the gripman is a warning to traffic, or is meant to demonstrate the gripman's talent at cable car bell ringing. Talent for bell ringing is rewarded at the annual cable car bell ringing contest held in Union Square in July.

The gripman's grip is the apparatus that clutches the cable running underneath the tracks (that's the whirring sound you hear). This cable travels continuously at 9½ mph over hundreds of pulleys spaced 15 feet apart. The gripping device is similar to a giant pair of pliers. For the car's forward motion, the gripman's job is to hold on to the cable.

The gripman's operating station has two foot pedals. One pedal operates the brake, a length of pine wood that is pressed against the track. On wet tracks the gripman has the option of stepping on the second pedal which releases sand onto the tracks causing extra friction for the brake. A brake lever is also used on the steep grades. An emergency brake is engaged by pulling a red-painted lever which drops a steel wedge down into the cable slot and quickly stops the car.

On Hyde Street between Lombard and Bay, the cable cars slide down a 21-degree slope. The conductor on the rear platform pulls his bar brake, and the gripman in front stands on his foot brake while madly sounding his bell for all the world to hear. The brakes pressed against the tracks create an aroma of burnt wood. This pleasant odor wafts across intersections at the bottom of a steep hill after a cable car descends. It's a treat that is pure San Francisco.

No matter where you begin your cable car adventure, there is a wide variety of rich experience to be enjoyed along the route—and a lot of it is free! Our cable car adventure begins at the turntable at Powell and Market streets. But before you board your cable car, let's take a look around the turntable.

The great cable car adventure begins at the Market Street turntable, near the foot of Powell Street.

THE POWELL–HYDE STREET LINE

#60 From Powell and Market Streets to Hyde and Beach Streets — Aquatic Park and Fisherman's Wharf

From the downtown turntable the cable cars begin their climb over the hills to the waterfront. Along the route they pass Union Square, Chinatown, and the Cable Car Barn before turning onto Hyde Street for the dramatic descent to Victorian Park.

Market Street Turntable

Visitors Bureau, BART, and landmark buildings

Market Street is San Francisco's Great White Way, the widest street in town which is all things to all people. Like the trunk of a tree, this is the main avenue from which most of the City stems. The cable car turntable at Market and Powell is a central plaza attracting a wide spectrum of people. On any given day, while you wait with the crowd for a cable car, you can see a cross section of the City's population passing by. Adjacent to the cable car turntable, down below the street level in Hallidie Plaza, you are likely to see a singing group or a jazz combo performing for little more than applause. This area around the cable car starting point is a people-watcher's paradise, where sandwich-board preachers proclaim the second coming beside a demonstration for women's rights, next to a shiny chrome machine that will stamp a penny into a souvenir for a quarter.

Market Street divides the hills from the valleys. It was laid out by one of the City's principal surveyors and early pioneers, Jasper O'Farrell, from Dublin. O'Farrell was a true visionary who wanted to create the American Champs Elysees, with the clock tower of the Ferry Building at the foot and a crown of formal rose gardens four miles west under Twin Peaks. The name Market Street was inspired by Philadelphia's Market Street.

In the 1880's transportation up Market was provided by a steam-engine train and a cable car line that branched out from East Street—now the Embarcadero—along the ship-crowded waterfront docks. In those early days San Franciscans who lived south of Market, the affluent part of town, were said to reside in Happy Valley. Town folks who lived north of Market called Happy Valley "south of the slot," referring to the Market Street cable car slot. Many San Franciscans still use the term today.

Over the years Market Street has gone through several transformations. The most recent was in the early 1970's when the BART subway project got started under Market Street. Older buildings were given a face lift, and the city fathers imported Mexican brick masons to lay red brick sidewalks. Sycamore trees were planted along the wide sidewalks, and major new construction mushroomed at the foot of Market Street, altering the City skyline.

Market Street Turntable ■ 9

One of the first Market Street beautification projects was inspired by the invention of electric streetlights. The Market Street light standards that resulted manifest the thinking of City officials at the turn of the century when, as Mark Twain observed, "existence was in the extreme and there was mediocrity in nothing." The top portion of these old street poles features a design that won a competition entitled "Path of Gold." The relief figures of Indians and covered wagons at the base of the polls, depicting the winning of the West, are a tribute to the '49er days.

Hallidie Plaza

Before starting off on your tour of the City, you may want to take advantage of the services of the **San Francisco Convention and Visitors Bureau (1)** in the lower level of Hallidie Plaza, adjacent to the entrance for the Powell Street **BART Station (2).** This office is open daily 9 A.M. to 5 P.M. and is a good source of free maps and guide brochures as well as more specific information. Ask for a MUNI map too. This map will help you connect the cable car lines with the city bus routes. On page 123 you will find a list of points of interest with a guide to help you find transfer points and bus numbers. Free transfers to bus lines and to the other cable car lines are available when you pay your 50-cent fare (exact change only). These transfers are available from the cable car conductor (and they make good souvenirs for the folks back home!).

The Convention and Visitors Bureau has several different phone numbers that you can call to find out what's happening around town. A two-minute recording summarizes the day's events: in English (391-2000), Japanese (391-2101), French (391-2003), German (391-2004), and Spanish (391-2122). For further information call: 626-5500.

Visitors from out of town who want to experience a ride on the BART (Bay Area Rapid Transit) trains may purchase a $1 ticket and travel the entire system for up to three hours, visiting any of the 34 uniquely designed stations. But you are required to enter and exit at the same station. BART runs Monday through Saturday, 6 A.M. to midnight, and Sunday 9 A.M. to midnight. The BART people suggest that, to avoid the rush-hour traffic, you should tour on the weekend or from 10 A.M. to 3 P.M. on weekdays.

Fifth Street crosses Market above Hallidie Plaza; one block south at Fifth and Mission is San Francisco's **Old Mint (3)**. This is a San Francisco landmark dating back to 1874; it's free and you shouldn't miss it. We like the Old Mint because a feeling of old San Francisco prevails, and because the specialty of the house is a glittering pyramid of gold ingots. Truly this is a grand and unusual sight: $9 million worth of 999.9 percent fine gold bars—41 bricks weighing 27 pounds each. Each ingot is valued at approximately $220,000. An additional 1,000 ounces of gold nuggets, some the size of hot cakes, are displayed with gold bricks to further tantalize you.

Just the knowledge of so much gold in one place is corrupting. Years ago a man in the hotel across the street was overcome with desire for some of the gold. He started a tunnel beneath the street with visions of coming up inside the gold room in the mint. But the heavy Fifth Street traffic above the tunnel proved his undoing. The vibrations caused a cave-in and effectively discouraged all future excavation efforts.

When the Old Mint was in full swing it stamped out gold coins at the rate of a million ounces a day. There was so much gold dust in the air that several enterprising workers made small fortunes by scrupulously cleaning their hair and clothes after each working day. A 4x6-foot rug that had graced the manager's office floor was found to contain nine ounces of gold dust when the operation was closed down in 1934. At that time the managers removed $2 billion worth of gold bars and shipped the treasure by rail to the new mint in Denver. The treasure train, well guarded by 175 policemen, required 25 trips to complete the transfer, which was accomplished without mishap.

In addition to the gold bars, the museum exhibits priceless gold clusters, including a 201-ounce gold crystal known as the Fricot Nugget. Also there for your inspection is a room filled with rare gold and silver coins under glass. Former mint offices display early American and forty-niner antiques, and there is a Numismatic Sales Room which sells mint sets of U.S. coins. Movies and lectures are also included in the Old Mint's daily program. The hours for the Old Mint are: Tuesday to Saturday, 10 A.M. to 4 P.M., closed Sunday and Monday. Admission is free.

At 898 Market Street, next to the cable car turntable, is a San Francisco classic well worth a walk through: **Woolworth & Co. (4)**, the largest of the old five-and-dime stores. It is filled with odds and ends, and the air is heavy with perfume. A 1930's lunch counter survives amid what seems to be general confusion. But it's fun looking for bargains and for things you don't need. According to one patron, the varieties of gumdrops and jelly beans alone are worth a trip all the way from Sacramento.

Woolworth & Co. is housed inside a fine example of old San Francisco architecture, the James Flood Building. This elegant gray lady has Renaissance/ Baroque ornamentation and adds much to the style of our City. The lobby is cavernous, elaborately constructed of marble and other fine quarried stone. The building also houses other commercial enterprises, as well as most of the Latin American consular offices.

The Flood Building serves as a monument to James Clair Flood, an Irishman–turned–San Francisco–pioneer who left quite a mark on our town. Flood and three other Dubliners, John William Mackay, the "Jolly Millionaire" William Shoney O'Brien, and James

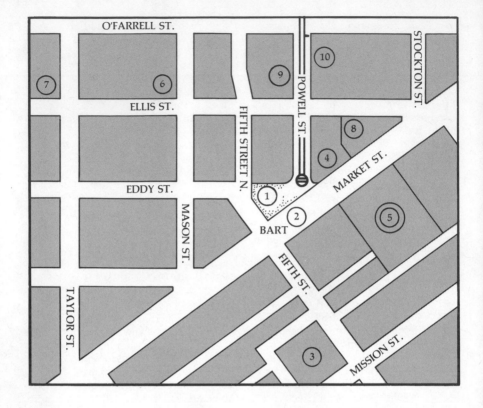

George Fair, struck it rich during the 1860's. Their collective Irish luck resulted in the richest strike of precious metal in American history: The Comstock Lode, in the Sierra Nevada foothills outside Virginia City. The Comstock mine bankrolled the building of the West and paid the boys from Dublin a million dollars a month for life. (One vein of silver and gold was 300 feet long, 1 foot thick, and 65 feet wide.) The mine continues in good health today.

There are numerous public clocks along Market Street. The one that is located in front of the Flood Building entrance has a touching story. The clock stands 30 feet high and was designed and constructed by Albert Samuels, a jeweler, and his friend, Joseph Mayers. Mr. Samuels wanted to leave his mark on this part of Market Street because he had spent his youth in the area. When the Panama-Pacific Exposition of 1915 opened in San Francisco on the northern shore of the City, Mssrs. Samuels and Mayers created the clock and installed it here as a contribution to the celebration of the new times.

Directly across the street from the Flood Building is the **Emporium Department Store (5)**. This is the flagship store in a chain of 12 around the Bay Area. The early California Supreme Court convened in this building until the 1906 earthquake and fire. After the fire the building was completely redesigned and rebuilt. A glass-and-steel frame dome roof crowns the store interior, casting soft warm light on the balconied sales floors and The Dome Cafe.

The cafe is open 11 A.M. to 4:30 P.M.; it serves cold lunches—salads, sandwiches, cheese, and wine. The Emporium is open Monday through Friday 10 A.M. to 9 P.M., Saturday 10 A.M. to 6 P.M., Sunday noon to 5 P.M.

A walk through this largest of the downtown department stores will reveal a note on the City's early days: the huge main floor columns are still dressed with gaslights. And on the third floor you can inspect at close hand a California Street cable car that stands forlornly on the public roof area.

The Market Street cable car turntable is at the foot of Powell Street, named after Dr. William J. Powell, who came to San Francisco as a young doctor on the 22-gun sloop-of-war *Warren*. The *Warren* was part of the American 1846 Pacific Squadron, under the command of Commodore John Sloat, which had taken California from Mexico and declared it United States territory. Another famous ship was part of that conquering fleet, the sloop-of-war *Portsmouth*. Today Portsmouth Square, site of the pueblo Yerba Buena (which grew to become the City of San Francisco), honors that vessel. It was a young lieutenant from the *Portsmouth*, Washington Bartlett, who was appointed mayor of the village which he renamed San Francisco. Mr. Bartlett gave fame to some of his fellow officers from the Pacific Squadron by naming streets after them, most notably, Montgomery, Dupont, Sloat, and Powell.

Both the #59 Powell-Mason line and the #60 Powell-Hyde line begin at the Market Street turntable and travel 11 blocks up Powell, passing over Nob Hill, before turning left on Jackson. Along this first part of the route are many points of interest. In this chapter we'll take you cross street by cross street, pointing out some interesting places you may want to explore.

Ellis Street

The Hilton Hotel, restaurants

Ellis Street is named for Alfred J. Ellis. A jack-of-all-trades, he panned for gold, walked a policeman's beat, and became a politician when the City was still young.

West on Ellis Street, between Mason and Taylor, is the **Hilton Hotel** (6). The largest hotel in the West, it offers a wide selection of restaurants. **Henri's Room at the Top** has a marvelous view of the Bay. Open at 11 A.M., with a buffet luncheon from 11:30 A.M. to 2 P.M. Dinner dancing after 6 P.M. Flaming dishes are the specialty of the **Chef's Table**, open for dinner, except Sunday, from 5:30 P.M. to 11 P.M. and for a la carte lunch Monday through Friday 11:30 A.M. to 2 P.M. The **Gazebo** is a family restaurant open for breakfast, lunch, and dinner, 6:30 A.M. to 1:30 A.M. Finally there's the **Cable Car Lounge**, open for cocktails 10 A.M. to 1:30 A.M.

When it's time to bid farewell to our town, you can catch a bus to the airport in the new **San Francisco Terminal** (7) at Ellis and Taylor, open 24 hours a day. Buses leave every 10 minutes from 6 A.M. to midnight and every 30 minutes from midnight to 6 A.M. The ride averages 30 minutes. Call 877-0345 for more information.

To the west of the Hilton Hotel is an area referred to as the Tenderloin. This is a section of town that offers more licentious forms of entertainment —topless saloons, adult bookstores, porno movie houses, and hookers. Proceed at your own risk.

Half a block east of Powell, on Ellis, is a real old-timers' restaurant and bar, **John's Grill** (8). This place, which comes close to capturing the atmosphere that prevailed in our City before

World War II, goes back to the fire and earthquake days of '06. The food and service are good, and the long bar is a place to see many of San Francisco's show business and political personalities.

Years back John's Grill was one of the haunts of author Dashiell Hammett, who wrote many books about the exploits of the fictional detective, Sam Spade. Hammett spent much time in John's Grill, doing character studies and writing notes for his stories. During the 1920's Hammett worked as a Pinkerton detective. The Pinkerton Detective Agency was upstairs above John's Grill. Hammett lived in a room at the Golden State Hotel down the street at the corner of Powell, until he moved up to Hyde Street on Russian Hill.

Devotees of Humphrey Bogart, Sydney Greenstreet, and Peter Lorre will remember the film, *The Maltese Falcon,* adapted from Hammett's story. Hammett memorabilia on display in the upstairs dining room of John's Grill includes the black falcon statuette, focus of the Hammett book. Prices are moderate to expensive. Open 11 A.M. to 2 A.M.; closed Sunday.

At 103 Powell, north of Ellis Street, is the **Captain's Wharf (9)**. This place will appeal to all who love the sea. Nautical artifacts create a salty atmosphere—brass lamps, ships' clocks and barometers, sea charts and books. There is much here to warm the blood and also induce a bit of sea fever. Open daily 10 A.M. to 10 P.M.

An excellent book shop that has continued in good health since the Gold Rush days is Books Inc., **Tro Harper's Book Store (10)** at 140 Powell. This is one of the West's oldest retail shops and one of the City's best. The store is well stocked with a large selection of fiction, nonfiction, and chil-

dren's books, as well as an extensive offering of maps and guides to California and the West Coast. Open Monday through Friday 9:30 A.M. to 9:45 P.M.; Saturday 9 A.M. to 7:45 P.M.; Sunday 10 A.M. to 5:45 P.M.

O'Farrell Street

Old-time restaurants and shops

Omar Khayyam's (11), 196 O'Farrell at the corner of Powell, is a well-known Armenian restaurant. During the late 1920's the spot housed a notorious speakeasy, "Coffee Dan's." George Mardikian, an immigrant dishwasher, worked there, dreaming of and working toward the day that he could have his own restaurant. After prohibition Mardikian took over the famous drinking spot and turned it into an excellent San Francisco eating palace. William Saroyan was one of Omar's frequent visitors. Generous portions of Tchakhokhbelli chicken and the popular shish kebab are all part of a long menu which will please anyone's taste. Open Tuesday through Saturday 11:30 A.M. to 10:30 P.M.; closed Sunday and Monday.

deserved reputation for Dover sole, but the European-trained chefs, Mr. Lew and Mr. Gigi, turn out Italian and continental food to equal most restaurants in the City. The rich and famous rank this place high on their list of San Fran-

Diagonally across the corner is a small piece of urban Americana that has survived the years and shouldn't be missed: **Marquard's Little Cigar Store** (12). It is a classic corner cigar and newsstand complete with a rare old iron sign in front. Besides magazines and newspapers, Marquard's also offers foreign cigarettes and cigars, postcards, pocket books, and candy. On the right day in the right kind of light, Marquard's looks like a scene out of old San Francisco. Open seven days a week 7 A.M. to 9:45 P.M.

Bardelli's (13), at 243 O'Farrell one block west of Powell, has a well-

cisco favorite dining spots. Open daily 11:30 A.M. to 10 P.M.; closed Sunday.

Planning to go to a party? The best place in the City to find masquerade materials, including masks, feathers, make-up, wigs, even ostrich boas, is at **Lew Serbin's Dance Art Company** (14) at 222 Powell. These people have the West's most complete stock of stage and costume materials. The store consists of two floors devoted to glittery things used to create party and costume fantasy. Open daily, except Sunday, 9:30 A.M. to 6 P.M.

A cable car crosses Geary Street on its climb up Powell Street past Union Square and the new Saks Fifth Avenue.

Geary Street (east of Powell)

Union Square and Maiden Lane

Union Square (15) has a fascinating history. John White Geary, on leaving the office of mayor, purchased the property at Union Square and deeded it to the City for use as a park. The land was a drab and wind-blown sand dune on the outer fringe of town. In time the sand dune was leveled, and the excess sand hauled down to the foot of Clay Street for use as bay fill.

Later, in the early days of the Civil War, John Geary distinguished himself as a major general on the battlefields of New Jersey, while the Union Army sympathizers in San Francisco held public rallies on the property he had turned over to the City. The name Union Square was a result of those early public meetings.

Years later, in July of 1898, San Francisco newspapers carried banner headlines proclaiming: "Admiral Dewey Ignores the Mailed Fist of The Kaiser, American Ships Hold Subic Bay." The Spanish-American War was ending and, as a tribute to Admiral Dewey, the monument that stands in the center of Union Square was unveiled.

These days Union Square serves as the main downtown City plaza. It is a favorite lunchtime gathering place that hosts orators of every kind, as well as street musicians and aspiring entertainers. The trees and shrubs cover a four-story underground parking garage connected by a tunnel to the St. Francis Hotel. With the backdrop of the elegant old hotel, there is a regal look to it all.

Public rallies, fashion shows, and speakers of every kind can always depend on a crowd in Union Square. Every year, in July, among the many year-round public events held here, there is a cable car bell-ringing competition which attracts thousands of people. Conductors, gripmen, and various personalities compete for a $2,000 prize.

This area is, for many San Franciscans, the center of the City. The best department stores, specialty shops, and hotels are close by. During the midday hour the beautiful people of our town surrender their automobiles to the Union Square Garage and file into the dozens of fine stores, restaurants, and popular rendezvous places found a few minutes' walk from this point.

If you plan to do some sightseeing by bus, you should check out the Gray Line Tours, one of the longest established tour groups in San Francisco. For your convenience a Gray Line Information Bus is parked at Union Square, on the corner of Geary and Powell. This company offers City tours as well as Chinatown tours; a nightclub tour; itineraries for the East Bay, Monterey Peninsula, and the wine country; and tours across the Golden Gate Bridge to Sausalito and Muir Woods.

A note for travelers who have arrived in the Bay Area by airplane: among the many store fronts facing Union Square you will find most national and international airline ticket offices. The Powell and Post street corner is occupied by **American Airlines (16)**, **British Airways (17)**, **C P Air (18)**, **Eastern Airlines (19)**, **United Airlines (20)**, **SAS (21)**, and **Mexicana Airlines (22)**. Facing the eastern border of Union Square you can find **Varig Airlines (23)**, **Pan Am (24)**, **TWA (25)**, and **Philippine Airlines (26)**.

Macy's (27), a few doors off Powell Street facing Union Square, is one of the City's more innovative department stores and one of our favorite shopping spots. This store has multilingual members on staff to help visitors with their shopping; they will even gift wrap and mail your packages. The store interpreters speak a total of 27 languages and will assist in posting letters, buying stamps, and purchasing money orders from the post office on Macy's cellar floor.

Macy's is also one of our City's most entertaining places to shop. There are eight floors, with every kind of merchandise. The Cellar, Macy's basement, is laid out as an arcade with gourmet shops and a Mama's restaurant (one of several in town) which serves delicious soups and salads, homemade breads, and desserts. During most days of the week the Cellar features food and kitchen equipment demonstrations. A luscious aroma lures you to the bakery shop with its pastry goodies, and there's also a wine shop. The book department on this same floor is one of the City's best, with a wide and up-to-date selection of the season's bestsellers and gift books. Macy's is open Monday through Friday 9:30 A.M. to 9 P.M.; Saturdays 9:30 A.M. to 6 P.M.; Sundays noon to 5 P.M.

On this same block is one of San Francisco's most exclusive fashion places, **I. Magnin (28)**, the white marble and black granite building at the corner of Stockton. In recent years Magnin's has added a ground floor men's department where one can find top designers well represented. The imported women's fashions, furs, jewelry, and cosmetics will please the ladies. Even the rest rooms are exclusive, with gold fittings. This is one of the few stores in town that have their own uniformed doormen. Open Monday, Thursday, and Friday 9:30 A.M. to

8 P.M.; Tuesday, Wednesday, and Saturday 9:30 A.M. to 5:30 P.M.; Sunday noon to 5:00 P.M.

The corner flower stands around Union Square are world famous. If you care to meet San Franciscans with a lot of character, talk to the flower-stand operators. They know the City well. One of them, Al Nalbandian, has been tending his flowers at the southwest corner of Geary and Stockton for 35 years. If Mr. Nalbandian reminds you of someone, look again; his face is famous. He travels to Hollywood on a regular basis to appear in movies as a bit player, and as a model in magazine ads.

Joseph Magnin (29), one block south, on the corner of Stockton and O'Farrell streets, has four floors of contemporary fashions for women and men. JM stores are found throughout the Bay Area and California. Open Monday, Thursday, and Friday from 9:30 A.M. to 9 P.M.; Tuesday, Wednesday, and Saturday 9:30 A.M. to 6 P.M.; Sunday noon to 5 P.M.

On the adjacent corner is **Liberty House (30)**. This store is a recent addition to the downtown shopping district. It carries quality women's and men's fashions as well as gourmet foods, liquors, luggage, and books, and has a good coffee shop in the basement. Open Monday, Thursday, and Friday 9:30 A.M. to 9 P.M.; Tuesday, Wednesday, and Saturday 9:30 A.M. to 6 P.M.; and Sunday noon to 5 P.M.

At 170 Geary is a long-established shop, the **Exclusive Cutlery Shop (31)**, with every kind of knife and scissors. You can even find left-handed shears. Open Monday through Saturday 9:30 A.M. to 5:30 P.M.

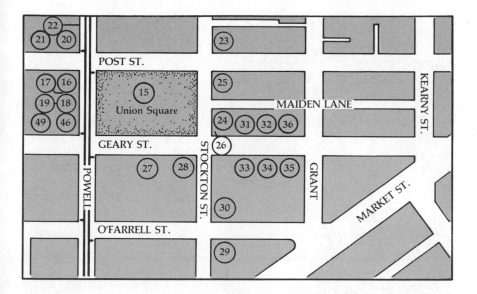

Britex Fabrics (32), at 146 Geary, carries one of the largest selections of fine fabrics in the Bay Area. We suggest you take a peek in here. All who appreciate fine woven fabrics from around the world will find this shop a marvelous place to spend some time. This 27-year-old family business has four floors which feature floor-to-ceiling racks of the finest domestic and imported silks, wools, cottons, and knits. If you appreciate quality, design, and color, Britex is a treasure house. Open daily 10 A.M. to 5:30 P.M.; Monday and Friday until 8 P.M.; closed Sunday.

Across the street is a branch of the very popular bookstore chain, **Waldenbooks (33)**, at 129 Geary. As is the case with all their stores, you can find most any of the leading books. Open Monday through Saturday 9:30 A.M. to 5:30 P.M.

If you prefer pearls you can find an unsurpassed collection of genuine and cultured pearls at the **Pearl Empire (34)**, at 127 Geary. Their salespeople, who speak five languages, specialize in hand-stringing pearls. Just looking at all the pearl rings is a rare treat. Open Monday through Saturday 10 A.M. to 5:30 P.M.

Morrow's Nut Shop (35), at 111 Geary, is a tiny shop that roasts up batches of fresh nuts to tempt you. We find it difficult to walk past this place without stopping to pick up a small bag of freshly roasted cashews. Open daily 9:30 A.M. to 5:30 P.M.; closed Sunday.

Close by, you are invited to inspect the dazzling elegance of fake diamonds. **The Whitehall Company (36)**, at 110 Geary, features a stone that has a hardness of 9 compared to a diamond's 10, reflects one-tenth of one percent less light than a diamond, and is far less expensive to buy. You can also find the real thing as well as genuine rubies, sapphires, and jade. Open Monday through Saturday from 9:30 A.M. to 5:30 P.M.

You'll find still more precious gems at **Granat Brothers (37)**, at the corner of Grant and Geary. They have a large selection of fine jewelry, including engagement diamond settings, wedding bands, as well as silverware and fine crystal. In addition to their jewelry design department, this store's specialty is imported and domestic watches and their repair. Open every day except Sunday 9:30 A.M. to 5:30 P.M.

At lunch time Maiden Lane becomes a shopping mall complete with outdoor cafes.

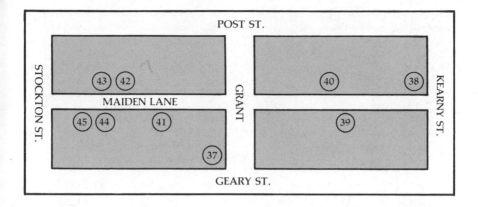

At the corner of Geary, head north up Grant Avenue; the next cross street is Maiden Lane. It runs for only two short blocks from the east side of Union Square.

Maiden Lane, which is situated between Geary on the south and Post on the north, used to be quite a notorious two-block-long alley. In the 1850's Maiden Lane was called St. Marks Lane, later Morton Street. But the people who lived there called it "Battle Row." It was two blocks of sporting houses—"debauchery, sin and depravity." The Row was ruled by the Spanish Kitten and her partner, the Boatswain. It was even more notorious than San Francisco's other midway of pleasure, the Barbary Coast, just over the hills on Pacific Avenue near the docks. After nearly half a century, retribution came to both the Row and to the Barbary Coast in the form of the 1906 earthquake and fire.

It was Albert Samuels, the jeweler, who suggested the present name to the City fathers. Both London and New York had named their diamond centers Maiden Lane, and the name seemed fitting for San Francisco as well. Everyone agreed. Today these two blocks and the adjoining area offer some of the City's finest stores. After the noon hour Maiden Lane is closed to auto traffic, restaurants set tables out, and the Lane becomes a sidewalk cafe. In the spring the area is festooned with daffodils and greens. In general the shops on Maiden Lane are open Monday through Saturday 9:30 A.M. to 5:30 P.M.

At the end of Maiden Lane, at Kearny Street, is **Brooks Cameras (38)**. This store is perhaps the largest downtown emporium dealing exclusively with the needs of photographers. Professionals and amateurs all gather here to inspect and purchase top-of-the-line photographic equipment from around the world. There are several other photo equipment stores located on the adjacent blocks of Kearny Street. Open Monday through Saturday 9 A.M. to 6 P.M.

Of all the jewelry stores in the area, one of the most unique is **Theodora (39)**, at 47 Maiden Lane. Theodora Scott has assembled a collection of classic, sophisticated pieces which have been designed by women for women. As a member of the American Gem Society, she offers fine diamonds set with a simple elegance that will never go out of style.

Across the street, at 50 Maiden Lane, is **Sergio Old Prints (40)**, which offers an excellent selection of old San Francisco prints and other Californiana. This shop also has a good collection of old maps, botanical prints, and Audubon prints. Sharing the space is another shop, **Paperworld,** which carries an exclusive line of executive and social stationery as well as custom invitations and desk accessories.

One of the early entrepreneurs on Maiden Lane was Ansel Robison, who founded **Robison's House of Pets (41)** at 135 Maiden Lane. Robison's father imported grocery items and sold them near the docks of East Street (the Embarcadero). Over the years the Robison family collected a considerable menagerie, picked up from sailors off the ships at the piers. Their green parrots, brown monkeys, and other animals roamed the store.

It was Mr. Robison's young son, Ansel, who had the morning chore of feeding the animals. He established the pet shop near the top of Maiden Lane soon after the 1906 fire and earthquake. The family business caters to animal lovers (some as far away as South America and Asia) who look to the Robisons to find pedigreed dogs and cats, or fine singing birds. Open daily 9 A.M. to 5:30 P.M.; closed Sunday.

Across the street is a building designed by Frank Lloyd Wright. The design is an early one that later became the inspiration for the Guggenheim Museum in New York City. Today the sign on the door reads **Helga Howie (42)**. This is the San Francisco headquarters of designer Rene Helga Howie, who is known for her work creating women's fashions of understated elegance.

Orvis (43), at 166 Maiden Lane, is a 200-year-old family business. They specialize in top quality fishing and hunting equipment along with related outdoor clothing, accessories, and gifts.

Looking for the latest in French fashions? **Andre Courrege (44)**, across the Lane, has them. This boutique features the designer's sweaters, skirts, and slacks, as well as his own brand of floral scents. In addition to Courrege's clothing and handbags for women, there is a traditional line of ready-to-wear imports from France for men. Open daily, except Sunday, 9:30 A.M. to 5:30 P.M.

Next door there is **Tennis Lady (45)**, a shop devoted to the needs of women tennis players of all levels.

Now let's head back across Union Square and explore the other side of Geary Street.

Geary Street (west of Powell)

*St. Francis Hotel and
the Theater District*

As you cross Union Square going west, the grand old building facing you at the corner of Geary and Powell is one of the finest hotels in the West, the **St. Francis Hotel (46)**. Like a grand dame, she welcomes you to San Francisco.

Since the beginning of the century this famous inn has been one of San Francisco's livelier and more romantic places. National and international personalities make this hotel their Bay Area headquarters. Royalty, politicians, heroes, the list of people who have stayed at the St. Francis is a roster of history. When a personage of high office is in attendance, the hotel is flag-draped and banners fly.

Union Square is a people-watchers' paradise where a wide spectrum of free entertainment is presented.

For many people the shrill whistle of the St. Francis doorman calling for a cab is as synonymous with San Francisco as the clanging of the cable car bells. And there's also an old expression for many San Franciscans: "Meet me under the clock at the St. Francis." The great magenta clock occupies a place of honor in the lobby, surrounded by the comings and goings of the international jet set.

Everything about the old St. Francis, including the staff, is first class. Today the hotel has 1,200 rooms, fine gourmet restaurants, ballrooms, meeting rooms, cafes, and cozy bars.

The English Grill in the St. Francis Hotel is a historic rendezvous. Here is old San Francisco atmosphere in the grand manner. If you feel flush and want to indulge yourself with good wine and marvelous cuisine, you should consider this place. Open for breakfast from 7 A.M. to 11 A.M., lunch 11:30 A.M. to 2:30 P.M., and dinner 5 to 10 P.M.; closed Sunday.

While you are in the St. Francis you might want to think about dinner at **Victor's,** at the top of the hotel on the 32nd floor of the new tower. The restaurant is named after a master chef, Victor Hirtzler, whose culinary arts were legendary just after the turn of the century. The atmosphere here is "relaxed posh," and there's a fantastic view of the City. Open every night, 6 to 11 P.M.; reservations are suggested; 956-7777.

Jacqueline St. Francis Perfume Shop, at 310 Geary near the hotel entrance, is without a doubt the best-stocked perfume emporium in town. They carry everything, all perfectly displayed row after row—it's an eye popper! Open Monday through Saturday 9:30 A.M. to 6 P.M.

Geary Street, west of Union Square, was known for many years as the street of theaters. Those were the days when John Drew, Otis Skinner, Minnie Fiske, Maude Adams, Henry Miller, Sarah Bernhardt, and so many other actors and writers were living and working in San Francisco. In those days there were more theaters along Geary Street than one can find today, but the memory lingers on. Today the programs at the Geary Theatre and the Curran Theatre continue to delight patrons. The street is still host to crowds attracted not only to the touring stage productions, but to many other interesting things along this historic avenue.

Lefty O'Doul's (47), at 333 Geary Street, is the creation of a native San Franciscan who played baseball for the Brooklyn Dodgers. During his heyday Lefty batted an average .368, and San Franciscans tried hard to have our Candlestick baseball park named O'Doul Stadium. Today Mr. O'Doul's corned beef and excellent hof brau-style lunches and dinners keep this Irish gentleman remembered in high esteem. In the evenings the sing-along piano bar is very popular. The walls of this Irish pub are decorated with a photo gallery of sports greats and guests from the past. Open daily from 11 A.M. till after midnight.

There is an excellent cafeteria on this block, **Mannings (48),** at 347 Geary Street. This popular downtown self-service restaurant has been in business here since just after the 1906 earthquake and fire. When you enter Mannings help yourself to a tray, then choose from a large selection of attractive and tasty dishes. We have never been dissatisfied. The doors open every day for breakfast at 6:30 A.M. and close at 9 P.M. A good value.

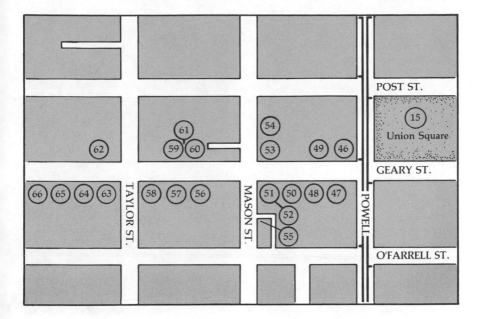

Rosebud's English Pub (49), at 370 Geary Street, is rich with English charm. It is popular with the theater crowds and downtown hotel guests. The emphasis is on elegance, with costumed waiters making a production out of everything served, from sandwiches to continental cuisine. Open Monday to Saturday 11 A.M. to 1:30 A.M., Sunday 3 P.M. to 12:30 A.M. Reservations are advised; 433-0183.

San Francisco is one of the few cities in the world where one can find jade in all hues. **Nina's Pearls and Jade (50)**, at 351 Geary, has an outstanding collection of gem jade in rings, necklaces, brooches, and earrings. Open daily, except Sunday, 10 A.M. to 6 P.M.

Close by, at 381 Geary, is **Vince's Jewelry (51)** with many fine imported items from China and South America. They pride themselves on their stringing work and fine jade carvings. Open 9:30 A.M. to 5:30 P.M.

A well-established art gallery in town is **Cory Gallery (52)**, at 377 Geary on this same block. They also have a gallery on Fisherman's Wharf; both feature contemporary and nineteenth-century artists. Open every day from 9 A.M. to 9 P.M.

Pam Pam East (53), on the corner of Geary and Mason, serves a large variety of delectable foods 24 hours a day. It is a favorite spot for breakfast or for an after-theater snack. We recommend their Belgium waffles.

Around the corner, at 420 Mason, is a theater with a permanent feature: **The San Francisco Experience (54)**, offering a 55-minute presentation with multiple slide and film projection, quadraphonic sound, and special effects to create a marvelous tour of San Francisco's past and present. While you wait for a performance to begin, you can play with old-time penny arcade gadgets or space age electronic toys. Performances are every hour on the hour from 11 A.M. to 10 P.M.

Delices de France (55), 320 Mason at the head of Elwood Lane, is a marvelous French brasserie, patisserie, and charcuterie, all in one. You can have an exceptional dining experience, either ordering from the kitchen or choosing food from the display cases which feature an irresistible array of such things as sausages, pate loaves, flaky pastries, and wines. Open at 9 A.M. Lunch from 11:30, and dinner at 6:30 with reservations requested: 433-7560.

Inside Elwood Lane is an excellent French restaurant with a plush, formal dining room. **La Bourgogne** is among the City's most revered restaurants. Dinner 5:30 P.M. to midnight; closed Sunday. Reservations are required, and you must wear a jacket and tie: 362-7352.

One of the country's best repertory companies is the American Conservatory Theatre, in the **Geary Theatre (56)** at 415 Geary. A.C.T. presents a long season of classic and contemporary plays. Tickets for all performances can be purchased at their box office at 415 Geary or by phoning 673-6440. Weekday performances at 8 P.M.; weekends at 8:30 P.M., with matinees at 2:30 P.M.

The best of Broadway is well showcased at the **Curran Theatre (57)**, 445 Geary. This theater has been host to the hottest productions—plays, ballet, light opera—since 1922. Ticket information is available at the Curran Box Office or by calling 673-4400.

The Four Seasons–Clift Hotel

According to *Harper's Bazaar*, the **Four Seasons–Clift Hotel (58)**, 495 Geary at Taylor, is one of about a dozen exceptional hotels in the world. The Redwood Room on the main floor offers superb dining in a posh and handsome setting. Lunch is served from noon till 2, dinner 6 to 11 with reservations: 775-4700.

Visitors take note: **Harold's** at 484 Geary, carries out-of-town newspapers as well as a large selection of American and European magazines. If Harold's doesn't have your choice of reading material, they can find it for you within a few hours. Open weekdays 9 A.M. to 9 P.M.; Saturday and Sunday 9 A.M. to 6 P.M.

After an evening at the theater or late at night, if you find yourself with a craving for a hot pastrami and cheese on New York rye and some good German beer, there are two places that can fill the need. Across the street from the Geary and the Curran theaters are two favorite San Francisco Jewish delicatessens: **David's (59)**, at 474 Geary, and the **Stage Delicatessen (60)**, at 418 Geary. David's was first on this block many years ago. His watchful eye for good food and service has made this deli and restaurant an outstanding success. Try the layered Belgian chocolate cake or thin cream cookies from David's bakers. Or take home one of his famous chicken liver sandwiches. The Stage opened for business after David's but has been equally successful, serving all kinds of tasty deli delights. There are huge rounds of cheese, smoked salmon, and all manner of salads behind the glass counters to tempt you. The beet borscht with sour cream is marvelous. The long menu of kniches and kishka will make any maven cry, and when you see the pastry tray you will know that West Coast delicatessens can equal those on the East Coast anytime. David's is open "at all the right times." The Stage Delicatessen "opens early and closes late."

If two delicatessens are not enough for you, there is an excellent soupery at 442 Geary. **Salmagundi (61)** is one of an international chain of soup restaurants. The offering here is three different soups each day from a repertoire of over two dozen varieties. For dessert you can choose from a number of superb chocolate goodies or have fruit and cheese. Open 11 A.M. to midnight.

The next block of Geary has two excellent book shops. **Albert Henry Books (62)**, at 524 Geary, carries one of the City's largest selections of paperback fiction as well as many hard-to-find domestic magazines and periodicals from Europe and Japan. Open seven days a week 10 A.M. to 11:15 P.M. The **Drama Book Store (63)**, across the street at 511 Geary, specializes in books on film, theater, and dance. Many books here are hardbound, and some are used. This is a small shop but one that is obviously managed by people who know and care about the theater. Open Monday through Friday 11 A.M. to 6 P.M.; Saturday to 8 P.M.

Two shops close by reflect the strong Scotch and Irish interests in San Francisco: the **Scottish Tartan Shop (64)**, at 515 Geary Street, with imports from Scotland, and the **Irish Castle (65)**, at 537 Geary. Both these shops have been here for many years and offer very good buys in linens, handmade shawls, and marvelous wool sweaters. You can also find books and records from Ireland. "May you live as long as you want, and never want as long as you live." Open 9 A.M. to 5:30 P.M.; closed Sunday.

The Jim Mate Pipe Shop (66), at 575 Geary, will be of interest to pipe fanciers. Mr. Mate is most fond of his imports of fine Amboselis, Dunhills, and Sasienis. His special blends of pipe tobacco are also distinctive. Open 10 A.M. to 5 P.M.; closed Sunday.

Post Street

Grand old clubs and distinguished shops

Post Street is named for Gabriel B. Post who arrived in San Francisco from the East Coast a few months after the Stars and Stripes had first been raised over the City. Mr. Post was an early member of the town council and later became a state senator. Post Street was a popular merchants' boardwalk beginning with the 1860's. Today many of the buildings along this avenue house some of the City's most elegant shops and private clubs.

The northern boundary of Union Square is Post Street. It is here, on the corner of Powell Street, that **Saks Fifth Avenue (67)** has chosen to erect its spectacular new West Coast headquarters. This company is well known for its designer collections as well as for quality ready-to-wear clothes and accessories. Saks has been a fashion leader in San Francisco for years. Open 9:30 A.M. to 7 P.M. on Monday; 9:30 A.M. to 5:30 P.M. Tuesday through Saturday; closed Sunday.

In keeping with this area's staid atmosphere is **John Howell Books (68)**, at 434 Post. One of the more distinctive book shops in town, it specializes in finely printed books by private presses and similar collectors' items.

Their selection of old California and San Francisco books is extensive. Mr. Howell grew up near the City and founded the *Daily Californian* at the University of California in Berkeley. His family carries on the store affairs these days. This book shop is the delight of book collectors around the country. Open 10 A.M. to 5 P.M.; closed Sunday.

The part of Post Street west of Powell has traditionally been the location of private clubs and professional offices.

The Olympic Club (69), at 524 Post, is a popular gathering place for San Francisco gentry. Until recently the City's business and social clubs were exclusively male membership. Today many of the old rules still stand, but here at The Olympic Club women have successfully stormed the ramparts.

The membership of the **San Francisco Press Club (70)**, at 555 Post, includes many of the City's journalists and other professional people. Politicians and public figures often speak here to test the local press on sensitive issues. Primarily the club serves as a good place in the middle of the City for the press to hide, and use the swimming pool.

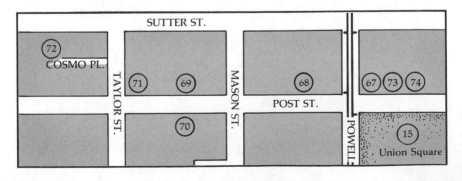

The **Bohemian Club (71)** is the ivy-covered building on the northeast corner of Post and Taylor. Founded by a group of artists and writers, it was dedicated to the "Burial of Care." Its membership has included Jack London, Frank Norris, and many of the City's other celebrated and elite. These days the "Owl's Nest," with its great bay windows facing Post Street, is a favorite vantage point in the club to look down on the City. So if you catch a clutch of men ogling at you from the corner windows, be assured it is merely a sport of long standing.

There might not be any "there" there, but Oakland did produce one of the best restaurateurs in the business, one Victor Bergeron, who presides over **Trader Vic's (72)** on Cosmo Place across Taylor from the Bohemian Club. The restaurant offers Polynesian and continental cuisine on a par with the best restaurants anywhere. Currently his Chinese oven barbecue beef is very popular, as is the seafood. The bar is popular for a rendezvous and a mai-tai with a friend. The waiters and all the staff are a devoted group. A dining experience here is a long-remembered pleasure. Open Monday to Friday 11:30 A.M. to 1 A.M., Sunday 4:30 P.M. to midnight.

We'll now return to Powell Street and explore the east end of Post Street.

In the Quantas Building, facing Union Square at 360 Post, is the **Redwood Empire Visitors' Center (73)**, a particularly good source of tourist information for anyone wishing to explore Northern California. They have a well-stocked rack of brochures on San Francisco, Marin, the wine country of Napa and Sonoma counties, the marvelous Mendocino coast and, of course, the Redwood Empire forests.

Take the elevator to the fourth floor. They will be glad to help you plot a great adventure north. Open Monday through Friday 9:30 A.M. to 5 P.M.

Next door is **Bullock & Jones (74)**, a fine men's store which carries the famed Burberry line of trench coats. The taste here is tweedy and conservative, and always classy. Open 9:30 A.M. to 5:30 P.M.; closed Sunday.

At the corner of Post and Stockton stands **A. Dunhill of London (75)**, one of the world's leaders in pipe and cigar supplies. They've been a tobacco emporium for 75 years, but now this company also makes and sells their own sports clothing for men, and also offers desk and office accessories and fine leather goods. Open 9:30 A.M. to 5:30 P.M.; closed Sunday.

Wedgewood Ltd. (76) is a small, stylish shop located at 304 Stockton, between Sutter and Post. This is the San Francisco headquarters for Wedgewood china from England, which manufactures tableware with an impeccable history that goes back two centuries. Open 9:30 A.M. to 5:30 P.M.

Around the corner, at 253 Post Street, is a branch of **Gucci (77)**, a world famous purveyor of fine leather goods: handbags, shoes, apparel, gifts, and luggage. Open 9:30 A.M. to 5:30 P.M.

Good ol' **American Express (78)** is located at 237 Post Street. For use as a traveling address, it always comes through. This office has a traveler's check dispensing machine for after-hours use, and during the normal workday it offers mail forwarding, tour services, and will take care of most travel arrangements. Open 9:30 A.M. to 5:30 P.M.; closed Sunday.

Gump's (79), at 250 Post, was established in the 1860's by two brothers who arrived in San Francisco from Heidelberg. This family business is well known by San Franciscans as a shopping place for quality contemporary craftsmanship in fine furniture, ceramics, home decorations and accessories. Perhaps even more famous is the Gump's third-floor Jade Room with one of the world's finest collections of jade in all its known colors and shades. Join the ranks of Sarah Bernhardt and Diamond Jim Brady by signing the guest book that includes Toscanini's signature inscribed next to a bar of music from Beethoven's Fifth Symphony. Open 9:30 A.M. to 5:30 P.M.

If you would like to spend some time making yourself beautiful, the very famous **Elizabeth Arden Salon (80)**, is located at 230 Post Street. Phone for an appointment, 982-3755.

Eddie Bauer Inc. (81) 220 Post Street, is a leader in top-of-the-line wilderness clothing and accessories. If you're looking for quality shirts or goose down jackets, parkas, and sleeping bags, they will outfit men and women for any expedition. Open 9:30 A.M. to 5:30 P.M.; closed Sunday.

At the corner of Post and Grant is **Brooks Brothers (82)**. This well-known New York clothing establishment has four floors stocked with everything for the well-dressed male; they also have a small women's department. The look here is conservative—English tweed and regimental stripes. Open 9:30 A.M. to 5:30 P.M.; closed Sunday.

Want to take in a ball game? Across the street at 170 Grant Avenue is the **Giants' Baseball Downtown Ticket Office (83)**. Besides tickets, they also carry Giant's baseball souvenirs: baseball caps, uniform shirts, jackets, and banners that make excellent gifts for just about everyone. Open 9:30 A.M. to 5:30 P.M.; closed Sunday.

Several firms in this neighborhood carry on the area's long tradition of offering quality gems crafted into fine gold and silver jewelry. These stores sell only the finest in craftsmanship, with unconditional guarantee; names like Gubelin, Omega, Tissot, Eterna, Vacheron et Constantin, Le Coultre, Piguet, and Milus are typical of the fine merchandise to be found here. Across Post Street on the corner of Grant you will see one of these stores. **Shreve & Co. (84)** offers the best in china, crystal, silverware, precious gems and metals. Open 9:30 A.M. to 5:30 P.M.; closed Sunday.

Before you continue down Post Street, we suggest a detour up Grant Avenue one block to Sutter Street, then back down the other side.

Half a block north on Grant is a historic alley called Tillman Place. A few steps inside the alley is a popular bookstore, Charlotte Newbegin's **Tillman Place Book Shop (85)**. Though the shop is small, the selection is excellent. Charlotte Newbegin is an important link in the long chain of San Francisco book people. Open 10 A.M. to 5 P.M.; closed Sunday.

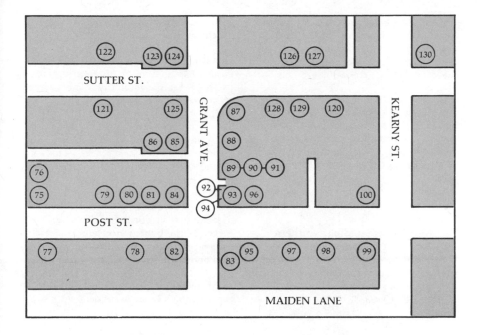

At the end of Tillman Place is a long-established watering hole and restaurant, the **Templebar (86)**. This is the oldest existing bar in the City and is watched over by a likeable Irishman, Mr. Guy Haines. Sons from the "old sod" have always been well represented in San Francisco; O'Farrell, Richardson, O'Brien, Flood, Fair, Haines—the list is long. Most of these gentlemen got their start behind a fine hand-carved bar similar to the rosewood antique found in the Templebar. This particular relic was shipped out from the East Coast around Cape Horn in 1856. Little has changed here over the years. Luncheon is served six days a week from 11:30 A.M. to 3 P.M., and generous cocktails are poured from 11 A.M. to 8 P.M.; closed Sunday.

For all golf, racquetball, baseball, and tennis players, there is a storeful of the best equipment at **Don Sherwood's Golf and Tennis World (87)**, 256 Grant. This store doesn't try to cover all sports, just those that involve knocking about a ball. Open daily, except Sunday, 9:30 A.M. to 6 P.M.

Tiffany & Company (88), 252 Grant, is known nationally for expensive, elegant jewelry. Press the button at the entrance and a uniformed doorman will usher you into the world of Tiffany's. In addition to the precious bijoux, we noticed a book for sale: *Table Manners for Young People*, at $1.95; perhaps we can all afford Tiffany's after all. Open Monday through Saturday 10 A.M. to 5:15 P.M.

Podesta Baldocci (89) florists, at 224 Grant, carry on a longtime San Francisco tradition of offering flower fashion for every occasion. During the holiday season this store consistently draws large crowds who flock to the beautiful window and interior displays for ideas and inspiration. Street musicians congregate here, too, adding to the season's spirit. Sightseers are welcome to wander around in the store's basement workrooms where nimble-fingered flower arrangers work amidst waist-high sacks of multicolored flowers. Open Monday through Friday 8 A.M. to 5:30 P.M., Saturday 8 A.M. to 5 P.M.

On the floors above this address is the **Stephen Wirtz Gallery (90)** which specializes in photography and paintings by nationally recognized artists. Shows in progress are announced with poster displays at the street entry. Open Tuesday through Friday from 11 A.M. to 5:30 P.M., and Saturday from noon to 5 P.M.

Also in this building, on the second floor, is **The Mountain Shop (91)**. This shop carries top-of-the-line products for mountain climbers—wilderness clothing, equipment, and supplies. Open daily 10 A.M. to 5 P.M.; closed Sunday.

Malm Luggage (92), at 222 Grant, is another long-established downtown business. For over a century they have provided fine leather products for business and travel. In recent years they have offered designer bags, wallets, and purses of every kind, as well as finely crafted luggage. Open daily, except Sunday, 9:30 A.M. to 6 P.M.

If you hunger for a delicious sweet about now, follow us to **The Candy Jar (93)**, at 210 Grant, for a rich and creamy chocolate truffle. San Francisco has several chocolate emporiums with tasty selections, but in our opinions this shop wins the chocolate kiss. This tiny but very successful hole-in-the-wall shop is run by a Hungarian, Maria Stacho, and her two lovely daughters. Every night the family gets together in their nearby candy kitchen and prepares the following day's supply: the largest bittersweet chocolate truffles in town—absolutely wonderful. Guaranteed to ruin a diet, but well worth it. Now properly fortified, you can pro-

ceed on your adventure. Open daily, except Sunday, 10 A.M. to 5:30 P.M.

Rupp & Taureck (94), at 208 Grant, has its own manufacturing facility in Germany where the owners create exclusive elegant knits and leather apparel for women. Other items for discerning women include scarves from the House of Christian Dior, and jewelry from Italy and France. This boutique enjoys an excellent reputation in San Francisco. Open daily 10 A.M. to 5:30 P.M.; closed Sunday.

Across the corner, at 187 Post Street, is the **Scotch House (95)**, which imports lambswool, cashmere, and shetland clothing from Scotland's finest knitters. These informal soft knits are ideal for foggy days in San Francisco. Open daily, except Sunday, 9:30 A.M. to 5:30 P.M.

One of the thrills of Christmas is the array of wonderful toys found in the displays at **F.A.O. Schwarz (96)**, 180 Post Street. For over 117 years this company has been known as one of the world's most complete and unique toy stores. The San Francisco shop is crammed with marvelous dolls from around the world, cuddly stuffed animals, miniature race cars, electric trains, model sets, and much more. This is a delightful, happy place to be. Open daily, except Sunday, 9:30 A.M. to 5:30 P.M.

Sidney Mobell (97), at 141 Post Street, is one of our City's most distinguished jewelers. In addition to finely designed jewelry, they carry most of the prestigious watch lines: Cartier, Rolex, Piaget, Corum, and Movado, to name just a few. Open daily, except Sunday, 9 A.M. to 5:30 P.M.

Mobilia (98), at 131 Post Street, offers fine Scandinavian furniture, functional Danish designs in golden teak and alderwood, soft leather sofas, and chrome and brass lamps. Open daily, except Sunday, 9:30 A.M. to 5:30 P.M.

At the end of this block, 101 Post Street at Kearny Street, is **Hastings (99)**, known for its quality men's and women's classically tailored suits and sportswear. Open daily, except Sunday, 9:30 A.M. to 5:30 P.M.

Across Post Street on the corner is **Livingston's (100)** handsome new department store which carries moderately priced women's apparel and accessories. Open Monday through Friday 10 A.M. to 6 P.M.; Saturday 10 A.M. to 5 P.M.

You may want to return to Powell Street by way of Sutter Street which is one block north. Fair warning: it is a long steep climb. For the sake of those who prefer to let the cable car do the climbing, we have started our tour of Sutter Street at Powell Street.

As the cable car climbs the Powell Street hill beyond Union Square, it passes another grand old San Francisco inn, the **Sir Francis Drake Hotel (101)**. The romantic tone of this hotel begins at the entrance with the doorman dressed in a bright red Elizabethan Beefeaters' costume. The hotel is, of course, named for Sir Francis Drake, the first Englishman to sail the world, who stopped off on the Marin County northern shore in 1573. The hotel maintains an Elizabethan elegance, and a nautical theme that seems in keeping with that old English sailor. The Drake offers several restaurants. **The Renaissance Lounge** serves an English tea between 3 P.M. and 6 P.M. **Drake's Tavern, a** small, intimate dining spot featuring continental cuisine, serves lunch Monday through Friday 11:30 A.M. to

2:30 P.M.; dinner 5 P.M. to 10 P.M.; cocktails 11 A.M. to 1:30 A.M. The **Carving Board,** known for its excellent roast beef, serves dinner from 5 P.M. to 10 P.M. The **Plate of Brasse,** the hotel's informal coffee shop, is open seven days a week from 6:30 A.M. to 10 P.M. Finally, there's the Drake Hotel's **Starlite Roof,** a popular nightclub with a reputation for its excellent rooftop view 21 stories above the City, which features a popular luncheon buffet and cocktail dancing after dark; Open Monday through Saturday 11 A.M. to 2 A.M. with dancing nightly from 9 P.M. to 1 A.M.; Sunday brunch is served 10 A.M. to 2:30 P.M.

The handsome **Chancellor Hotel (102)**, across the street, was constructed soon after the 1906 earthquake and fire. The buildings in this neighborhood were constructed after the devastating fire that burned most of the town as far west as Van Ness Avenue. The accommodations at the Chancellor Hotel are large and well cared for, and have a luxury not found in most modern hotels. There are large bathtubs, thick towels, and well-lighted rooms, and the service is first rate.

Sears Restaurant (103), at 439 Powell next to the Chancellor Hotel, is a popular old San Francisco place which always seems to be filled with satisfied customers. Open for breakfast and lunch, the restaurant is usually crowded with waiting patrons. But as the famous Boston Pops orchestra leader, Arthur Fiedler, who was a regular at the Chancellor Hotel and dined at Sears often, said: "The wait at Sears is worth it." The prices are quite reasonable, and the featured 18 pancakes served with the traditional fixings are a San Francisco favorite. Open Wednesday through Sunday, 7 A.M. to 2:30 P.M.

Shop windows on Sutter Street are generally marvelous creations in their own right.

Sutter Street

*Art and antiques,
exclusive boutiques*

Sutter Street honors the memory of one of the City's early pioneers, John Augustus Sutter. The name Sutter is immediately associated with gold — the gold found at Sutter's Mill near Sacramento. That discovery started the Gold Rush of 1849 and the migration of thousands of people to California. It was James Marshall who first picked up a nugget of the gold metal on Sutter's property in January 1848. Later, Sam Brannan, the Mormon leader, announced Marshall's discovery in San Francisco; he displayed a glittering sample to an evening crowd at Portsmouth Square, and the rush was on.

The historic event was recorded by the San Francisco newspaper, *The Californian,* on page two of the eight-page newspaper, on Wednesday, March 15, 1848: "Gold Mine Found. In the newly made raceway of the saw mill recently erected by Capt. Sutter, on the American Fork, gold has been found in considerable quantity. One person brought thirty dollars worth to New Helvetia. California, no doubt, is rich in mineral wealth; great chances are here for scientific capitalists. Gold has been found in almost every part of the country."

Today Sutter Street offers many interesting places to stop. San Franciscans know this street for its array of exclusive boutiques and art galleries, antique shops, excellent bookstores, and more.

Travelers from Europe will appreciate the store at the corner of Sutter and Powell: the **International Corner** (104), a bookstore with a large selection of German, French, and Spanish newspapers and magazines. This is also a good place to find foreign language maps, guidebooks, and other useful information for people from overseas. Open daily, except Sunday, 9 A.M. to 10 P.M.

Art galleries abound on the first few blocks west of Powell: **Pasquale Iannetti Gallery** (105), **Gallery One** (106), **Swanson Art Gallery** (107), **John Pence Gallery** (108). They feature the work of artists with international reputations — Picasso, Chagall, Calder, Miro — as well as the emerging talents of the art world. Other shops along here offer antique art treasures, antique jewelry and furniture, cooking utensils, fine fabrics, Oriental rugs, books, and toys.

The White Duck Workshop (109), at 517 Sutter, is a boutique for "state of the art" clothing with a Far Eastern flavor. Their exclusive appliqued velveteen jackets, jumpers, and dresses are simple yet elegant for day or evening; a garment from White Duck will be cherished for a lifetime. Open 9:30 A.M. to 5:30 P.M.; closed Sunday.

The 500 block of Sutter has a clutch of shops that reflect the European heritage found in San Francisco.

Pierre Deux Original Fabrics (110) is an establishment with roots in the French countryside. The owners have brought together a sizable collection of French provincial cotton yardage and many unusual cotton borders. If you can't sew a stitch, don't despair; they also carry an array of ready-made pillows, pot holders, wallets, aprons, etc. Open daily, except Sunday, 9:30 A.M. to 5:30 P.M.

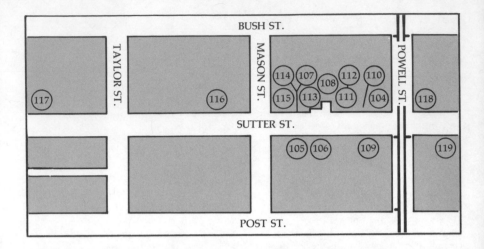

Close by is the **John Simmons Store (111)**. Once a two-story home with a tiny inner courtyard, this shop offers a change in pace from department store shopping. It is a French gift boutique which carries dinnerware, cutlery, and marvelous one-of-a-kind items. A large red macaw from the wilds of Brazil, who answers to the name of "Florida," rules the roost from his cage at the back of the store. Open daily, except Sunday, 9:30 A.M. to 5:30 P.M.

Upstairs in the same house is a tiny boutique called **Obiko (112)**. This shop represents 12 Bay Area designers of women's informal and formal wear, all with a distinctive Far East flavor. The owners refer to their many unique offerings as wearable art. Open daily, except Sunday, 10 A.M. to 6 P.M.

La Ville du Soleil (113) takes a novel approach to displaying French countryside cooking utensils and hand-crafts, toys, French dinnerware, linens, willow baskets, and hand-knit woolen sweaters from the provinces. Everything is attractively set in the atmosphere of an authentically reconstructed French mid-19th century village shop.

Cooking utensils for the most discriminating of cooks can be found at the **Williams-Sonoma Kitchenware (114)**. Stainless steel, copper, wood, and glass, plus a large array of sophisticated and time-tested kitchen aids for the home chef. Open daily, except Sunday, 9:30 A.M. to 5:30 P.M.

At the top of the block is **Stewart's Treasure House (115)**, a marvelous shop featuring antique jewelry. Three generations of Stewarts comb West Coast estate sales to find antique items of rare quality. The Stewarts offer other gift items, but it is the window display of gold chains and rings that always seems to draw a group of admiring oglers. For those seeking precious stones and metals set in styles from the past, this shop offers quality, reasonable price, and integrity. Open daily, except Sunday, 10 A.M. to 5 P.M.

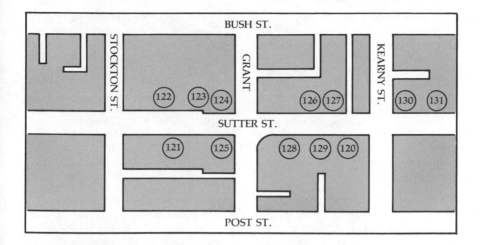

Farther up the street, in the middle of the block, is the **YWCA (116)**, at 620 Sutter. Inside, to the right of the main entry, is **The Cookbook Corner,** a bookstore well worth a stop. Shop owner Taya Monfried carries hundreds of fine and unusual cookbooks, one of the best selections in the City. Taya travels around the country seeking out new and out-of-print cookbooks to offer her customers. Open daily, except Sunday, 9:30 A.M. to 5:30 P.M.

We have a favorite restaurant, in the next block at 750 Sutter, for lunch, dinner, or Sunday brunch. Dining at **Lehr's Greenhouse (117)**, is like dining in an arboretum. Customers relax in white wicker chairs surrounded by flowers in bloom, a profusion of green plants, and indoor fountains. The menu is creative, the food excellent, the portions generous, and the atmosphere always enjoyable. The dinner restaurant features cosmopolitan cuisine and an array of delicious desserts. Open from 11 A.M. to 4 P.M. and from 5 P.M. to 10:30 P.M. The Sunday brunch, which is something of a San Francisco tradition, begins with Ramos fizzes at 9:30 A.M. and goes until 2:30 P.M.

Walking in the opposite direction, east from the cable car stop at Sutter and Powell, you'll also find a great deal of shopping and wonderful dining opportunities.

One of the several Holiday Inn hotels to be found in downtown San Francisco is the **Holiday Inn, Union Square (118)** on the corner of Powell and Sutter. It offers several restaurants and a penthouse pub.

An interesting and innovative display of San Francisco architecture is the 450 Sutter Medical Building. Some people refer to it as the Ill Building. This structure has been labeled as an important example of Modernist architectural design. It was one of the first to incorporate a parking garage with interior shops and services. This building was one of San Francisco's early skyscrapers, and in its day it was the largest medical building in the world.

Those with an appreciation for large and well-stocked toy and hobby shops will like two stores close by. At 445 Sutter is **Jeffrey's Toys (119)**, part of a San Francisco chain of four stores. This particular shop carries model kits and accessories, ships and airplanes, and military equipment. Several floor-to-ceiling glass cases display whole armies of lead soldiers from France and England. Hundreds of other imported miniatures make this a must stop for youngsters of every age. Open daily, except Sunday, 10 A.M. to 5:30 P.M.

An equally fascinating toy shop two blocks down, at 217 Sutter, is **The Hobby Company (120)**, which carries radio-controlled airplane models and accessories as well as miniature military models and most hobby supplies. Open Monday through Friday 9:30 A.M. to 6 P.M., Saturday 10 A.M. to 5 P.M.

The Magic Pan (121) restaurant, at 341 Sutter, offers a large selection of tasty French crepes filled with vegetables, seafood, or fresh fruit. Open daily, except Sunday, 11:30 A.M. to 10 P.M.

One of the City's fashion leaders is **Wilkes Bashford (122)**, at 336 Sutter Street. The store is known for quality and excellence of design in both men's and women's clothing—everything from contemporary designer sportswear to formal attire. Open Monday to Saturday 10 A.M. to 6 P.M.

Michael's Artist & Drafting Supplies (123) at 314 Sutter is a well-stocked art supply store. This shop services San Francisco's large and talented graphic arts industry. The City has a long tradition as a printers' town. Open daily, except Sunday, 9:30 A.M. to 5:30 P.M.

Caravansary (124), 310 Sutter Street, was originally a gourmet gift shop featuring quality kitchenware as well as imported coffee, tea, fine wines, and cheeses. This shop has grown to include a mezzanine espresso bar and a fine restaurant on the second floor. The Armenian and continental cuisine features lamb and chicken dishes prepared from recipes that are centuries old. The gourmet shop and espresso bar are open daily except Sunday 10 A.M. to 5:30 P.M. The restaurant serves lunch daily from 11 A.M. to 3 P.M. and dinner from 5 P.M. to 10 P.M.; closed Sunday. Dinner reservations are advised; 362-4640.

Notice the interesting building on the southwest corner of Sutter Street and Grant Avenue. This is yet another San Francisco classic, a lovely example of early 1890's architecture that goes largely unrecognized by the public. The building was prefabricated in cast iron on the East Coast, then shipped to California via Cape Horn in 1906. The original owner wanted the building as a West Coast diamond headquarters, part of San Francisco's new Maiden Lane. The ship bringing the building, in pieces, from Baltimore was held up by bad weather and arrived in the Bay the day of the big earthquake and fire. Today the building houses **Paul's Antiques (125)**, three floors full of antiques. At the corner entrance there is a ground-floor snack bar and sandwich-to-take-out shop, and a newsstand. Open 9 A.M. to 7:30 P.M.

Fine cooking utensils are one of the specialty items for which Sutter Street is known.

Another Sutter Street art supply store is **Flax Art Supply Company** (126) at number 250. This is a wholesale and retail business with a large inventory of domestic and imported art materials. If Flax does not have what you need in stock, they will find it for you; they can if anyone can. Open 9 A.M. to 5 P.M.

For fine craftsmanship in traditional and classic furniture we suggest a stop at **W & J Sloane Company** (127), 216 Sutter. The name Sloane goes back to the pioneering days of California. This store houses seven floors of fine furniture and room accessories. Open daily, except Sunday, 9:30 A.M. to 5:30 P.M.

Across the street is **The White House** (128). Presently waiting for a new owner, the building once housed a famous San Francisco department store. The store opened for business in 1885 as a dry goods shop and quickly grew to one of the most important department stores in the West. A White House label in a piece of clothing was treasured as a proof of quality. In 1965 the White House name faded into the City's past.

Two excellent bookstores can be found just a few steps away. **Brentano's** (129) at 265 Sutter carries a large selection of gift books. The extensive paperback book section is on an upstairs mezzanine floor; a used book department is in the basement. Open daily, except Sunday, 9:30 A.M. to 5:30 P.M.

At the corner of Kearny and Sutter is **B. Dalton Bookseller** (130). This is the main San Francisco store in a large nationwide chain. The selection of hardbound and trade paperback books is extensive, covering most new publications from publishers on the East and West coasts. This store also carries a good selection of business and craft books. Open 9:00 A.M. to 5:45 P.M.; closed Sunday.

A few doors east at 130 Sutter is the Hallidie Building, named after the cable car inventor. (There is no San Francisco street named for Mr. Hallidie). Like the cable car, this building, with its "glass curtain walled" facade, was an innovative first for the City. It was constructed as the San Francisco office for the Regents of the University of California. The **Sutter Station Post Office** (131) is on the ground floor.

The pagoda gate at the corner of Grant Avenue and Bush Street marks the entrance to Chinatown.

Chinatown

Bush Street and up Grant Avenue

In the middle of the cable car's climb up to Nob Hill, it stops at Bush Street. Chinatown starts two blocks east at Bush Street and Grant Avenue and continues parallel to the cable car line for more than six blocks. Cable car conductors often suggest that passengers enter Chinatown at Washington Street or Jackson Street. That is certainly one way, but we think that in order to capture the real flavor of *Gum San Ta Fow*, "the big city on the golden hill," one should enter by way of Grant Avenue through the Chinese Gate at Bush Street. Chinatown may have its eyesores, but they are redeemed by its lovelier places, and the Chinatown Gate is one of them.

On Bush Street, just before you reach Grant Avenue, you'll pass the excellent **Sierra Club Bookstore (132)** at 530 Bush. Next door is one of the better craft galleries in town, **Contemporary Artisans (133)**. Both are open daily, except Sunday, 10 A.M. to 5 P.M.

At the corner of Grant you will see the magnificent **Pagoda Gate (134)**, entrance to the largest Chinese settlement inside the United States. This imposing structure was a gift to the City of San Francisco from the government of Taiwan. When construction started, in the late 1950's, relations between China and the United States were at a low ebb. The gate was finally dedicated in 1968.

Many of the shops along Chinatown's Grant Avenue carry the usual trinkets and tourist merchandise. Yet behind what appears to be gaudy clutter there are quality goods, and much fun and adventure to be discovered.

San Francisco's historic Chinatown dates from the Gold Rush days of 1849, when Chinese laborers were imported from China's port city of Canton to work in the gold fields. Later, Chinese were the main labor force for the building of the transcontinental railroad. The first Chinese to arrive, two men and a woman, sailed into San Francisco Bay on the brig, *Eagle*.

The neighborhood around Portsmouth Square (between Clay and Washington streets) was the location of the earliest Chinese settlement. Sacramento Street, three blocks north of the Chinatown Gate, was "Little China," and the street itself is still referred to as *Tong Yan Gai*, "Chinese Street." Adjacent to the Chinese settlement on the east side was "Little Chile," which was known for a while as "Sydney Town," and later became the infamous "Barbary Coast." Today, it is Jackson Square, an enclave of lovingly restored brick alleyways and courtyards lined with classy decorator showrooms and antique shops. Before the 1906 earthquake and fire, Grant Avenue was named Dupont Street and was the main Chinatown thoroughfare. Today many Chinese people continue to refer to the street as *Dupont Gai* (old Dupont Street).

It was not until the 1920's that first-class citizenship was granted to the Chinese population of America. In most cases, the Chinese did not care. They had come to America to build their nest eggs and return home. A few thousand dollars was a fortune in China, enough for a whole family to retire. But the culture those first Chinese immigrants established here grew to be permanent, and businessmen in China soon recognized San Francisco as an important export market. Today Chinatown offers choice value not found even in China. Our Chinatown is rich and full of rare and exotic treats affordable only in this country. As many Chinese people will acknowledge, the best of China's haute cuisine and craftsmanship is right here in San Francisco.

It is important to keep in mind that in order to receive full value from your adventure in Chinatown it is necessary to be "deserving"—at least for the Chinese clerks to think so. A show of respect and appreciation may move a shop owner to show you his prized possession. If a customer is deserving and worthy, the rare antiques come out of the backrooms, and the *haute cuisine de maison* is suddenly available at any hour. Show your interest. Haggle. Do not be timid to look around; it is expected. Generally the second-floor showrooms, the quieter recesses, are where you will make your Chinatown discoveries.

Chinese craftsmanship has a tradition of excellence. Teakwood and rosewood, petit-point footwear and handbags, silk kimonos, porcelain, pearls, precious stones, and brasswork—and a great deal more—are all found in Chinatown. Wonderful odors hang in the morning air. The smells of teakwood and fresh fish mingle with the singsong sounds of Chinese conversation and cries of ducks and chickens. It is an ancient formula to make your visit to Chinatown a memorable highlight of your holiday.

For leisurely strolling through the streets of Chinatown, we recommend the morning hours when the Chinese community is just beginning its work-ing day. These are the hours when the herb shopkeepers lay large round rattan trays of lizard skins, seaweed, and roots along the sidewalks to catch the morning sun. These are the hours when you will see trucks at street corners selling fresh vegetables, live ducks and chickens to local residents. We also like the hours just after sunset when the streetlights come on and the neon lights of the shops and restaurants turn Grant Avenue into an exotic fairyland. Chinatown is a sensual experience you will long remember.

City of Hankow Tassel Company (135) is the first building to the right as you enter the Chinatown Gate. This is as close as you'll come to a Chinese department store. It offers two floors of handcrafted teak and rosewood linen chests, tables, lamps, and rattan furniture, as well as an excellent assortment of Chinese fabrics, hardware, clothing, and gifts. Open Monday through Saturday 10 A.M. to 9:30 P.M.

On the opposite side of the street West meets East head-on in a western clothing shop called the **Indian Trading Post (136)** at 527 Grant. Three doors up the avenue is a Chinese disco nightclub, **The Ricksha (137).**

Jade rings, necklaces, and earrings are all available in the Chinatown jewelry stores found along Grant Avenue and many side streets. The Chinese consider jade to be one of the most valuable gemstones. Because of the large Chinese population in San Francisco, the selection of fine jade here is excellent. Apple-green jade is most prized by collectors; it also brings the best price. Stay away from the army fatigue colors of green jade. A leafy green color is what the expert looks for when considering value. Jade can also

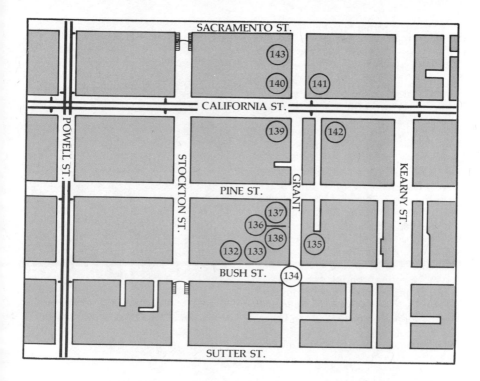

be found in many other hues—apricot, lavender, white, and purple. Most of the jewelry shops also offer values in pearls, as well as sapphires, opals, lapis, amethysts, topazes, tourmalines, garnets, emeralds, coral, and rubies.

There are still a few choice Old China pieces of porcelain to be found in Chinatown. The blue-smocked proprietors of the **City of Shanghai (138)** at 519 Grant can occasionally be talked into showing you the rare Ming and Kang-si porcelains they keep secreted away for special customers. They also pride themselves on their large selection of petit-point handbags, embroidered linens, and lace, as well as bolts of silk brocade. The clerks will take your order for a fine silk *kimona* or a *cheong-sam*—the traditional close-fitting Chinese dress. Open Monday through Saturday 9 A.M. to 5:30 P.M.

Two traditional Chinese buildings loom prominently at the corner of California and Grant Avenue. These buildings were designed to be the focal point for an intended model "Oriental City" after the 1906 fire. The building on the southwest corner houses the popular **Yamato Sukiyaki House (139)**, 717 California. Across the street is the **Chinatown Wax Museum (140)**, at 601 Grant. If you don't let the window displays of old dried snakes and lizards in bottles of liquid scare you away, you'll find some fascinating highlights of ancient Chinese history inside—from Chinatown torture scenes to the splendor of Marco Polo's visit to the court of Kublai Khan. Open daily 10 A.M. to 11 P.M. Admission is $1.50.

The California Street cable car line crosses Grant Avenue midway up the long California Street hill. The cable cars rumble to a stop in front of a red brick church at the corner of California and Grant. It is **Old St. Mary's (141),** the number two historical landmark in San Francisco. The Chinese call this church *Dai Choong Low,* "the tower of the big bell." The words under the clock on the bell tower read: "Son, observe the time and fly from evil" (from Ecclesiastes V, XX). The church was built in 1854 as the first Catholic cathedral in the City. It was damaged in the 1906 earthquake and fire, then restored to its original state. A Sunday mass here is very special. The organ is considered to be of rare sound quality, so much so that touring organists with outstanding talents frequently give programs here for the general public just for the opportunity to play the organ. Mass is held every day, and a special folk mass is celebrated each Sunday at 5 P.M.

Chinatown takes on a whole new dimension after dark.

Across California Street is **Old St. Mary's Park (142).** The alley at its side, bordered with tall poplar trees, is Quincy Street. The park is the landscaped roof of a garage, but you would never know it. There are many large flowering trees and a well-kept green lawn. This oasis in the middle of downtown makes a perfect place to have a take-out lunch break. Chinatown is loaded with take-out food shops, so keep this park in mind. The view of the downtown financial district with its high-rise buildings is outstanding, especially at night.

Beniamino Bufano, a well-known San Francisco sculptor, presented the Catholic fathers of Old St. Mary's Church with the magnificent stainless steel and granite statue of Dr. Sun Yat-sen which stands in the middle of the park. Sun Yat-sen's counterpart in American history would be a hero on a level with George Washington.

Not far from the park, at 631 Grant, is the **Far East Cafe (143),** a favorite lovers' rendezvous for many years. A waiter will meet you at the entrance and escort you down a narrow hallway to your own private room, complete with curtained doorway. Good food, moderately priced, and so romantic. Open 11:30 A.M. to 11:30 P.M.; closed Monday.

During your walk along the back alleyways and side streets of Chinatown, listen for the whirring sounds of sewing machines. These sounds are coming from small storefront shops. The windows of these shops are usually covered over with Chinese newspapers, but the doors are generally open. Inside you can see Chinese women sewing pre-cut garments for major West Coast clothing manufacturers. A number of these shops can be seen along Powell too. Chinatown has close to a hundred. Most are illegal, but they are the only source of income for many families. Late at night many of these shops are still going full speed.

Another sound that you can hear in Chinatown, mostly at night, is the click-clicking of Mah-Jong tiles. This traditional Chinese game is played in numerous private clubs and Chinese benevolent associations; several are along Waverly Place.

Waverly Place is one block west, uphill, from Grant Avenue, between Sacramento and Washington streets. This alley is a favorite Hollywood movie location for shooting scenes that need an intriguing Oriental atmosphere. It is also a good place to shoot your own photos with an authentic Chinatown background.

The **Tien Hau Temple (144),** at 125 Waverly Place, is said to be the oldest of its kind in the United States. The main altar of gold holds an image of the Queen of Heaven, Tien Hau. This is the goddess of sailors, who aids all travelers on the sea. The temple was built in gratitude by the Chinese immigrants who arrived in America from China after a long and hazardous crossing of the Pacific. Open daily 10 A.M. to 5 P.M. and 7 P.M. to 9 P.M.

Chinese temples are sometimes called "joss" houses. The word is a corruption of "boss" and "god." The higher the joss house stands physically, the closer its altar is to heaven. In Chinatown you can find several temples elevated to the highest point possible; some are on the top floors of tall buildings.

The **Kong Chow Temple (145)** is on the fourth floor at 855 Stockton. This temple is managed by the Kong Chow Benevolent Association, a member of the powerful Chinese Six Companies. The temple rituals are carried out with the aid of many priceless gold items available for your inspection. Open daily, 10 A.M. to 3 P.M.; closed Monday.

The next alley west, running parallel to Waverly Place, is Spofford. This is yet another favorite Hollywood filming area. The building at 36–38 Spofford was the **residence of Dr. Sun Yat-sen (146)** during the time he is said to have plotted the Chinese revolution of 1911. The Chinese community know this alley as *Sun Louie Sang Hong,* "New Spanish Alley." After the 1906 earthquake and fire, Spanish Alley was a street of bordellos with a Mexican and South American clientele. At the corner of Spofford and Washington Street is the **Kwan Yin Temple (147)** which houses the spirit of the goddess of mercy, Kwan Yin.

Just north of Spofford Alley is the Old Chinatown lane, *Mar Tong Hong,* or "Horse Stable Alley," formerly Cameron Alley. The whole area makes an excellent background for photography.

As you walk from these back alleys look around you and you will see that there are many restaurants to choose from. The menus offer everything from an American-style breakfast to a 15-course Chinese banquet. If you are unfamiliar with Chinese food you may want to test it out first. Try a *char sui bow,* a steamed bakery bun filled with tasty roast pork and sauce, or a Chinese custard tart. Children will enjoy ginger candy, which also makes an unusual gift for friends back home.

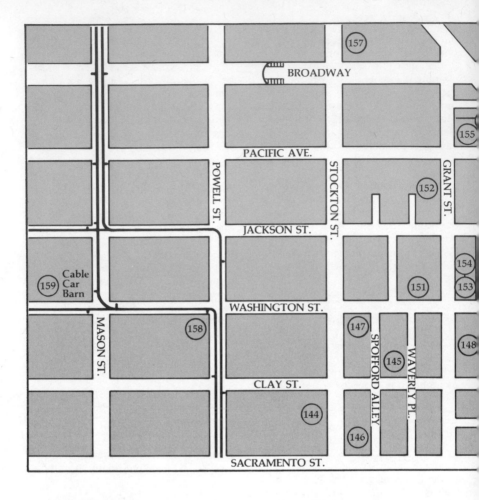

Cooking traditional Chinese cuisine requires the use of a wok, a deep round pan that is large enough to contain all the vegetables and many other ingredients used in Chinese recipes. The shops along Grant Avenue carry woks along with many other interesting and useful utensils for the kitchen. The small grocery stores in Chinatown carry all the ingredients you'd need to make your own Chinese dinner. The same grocery stores also carry bags of Chinese fortune cookies which make great gifts.

One of the most elegant restaurants in Chinatown is the award-winning **Empress of China (148)**, at 838 Grant Avenue. Dine on the sixth floor overlooking Portsmouth Square, surrounded by the splendor of the Han Dynasty. Open for lunch and dinner, 11:30 A.M. to 11 P.M.

territory. One of Montgomery's officers, Lieutenant Washington Bartlett, was appointed mayor, and the town was in business.

A main path out of town, named *Calle de Fundacion* (Founding Street), skirted the top of the plaza. Two more paths, Clay and Washington streets, led down to the cove where an occasional transport ship picked up cargoes of hides and tallow, California's principal exports at the turn of the century. *Calle de Fundacion* was renamed Dupont Street by the town's new mayor to honor Captain Samuel Dupont of the sloop-of-war *Cyane*. Half a century later, when President U. S. Grant died in 1908, Dupont Street was renamed Grant Avenue.

A rather lost and pathetic 9x10-inch bronze plaque set into the wall of 823 Grant Avenue marks the birthplace of the City of San Franicsco. It reads:

> "Here, June 25, 1835, William A. Richardson, founder of Yerba Buena, later San Francisco, erected its first habitation, a tent dwelling, replaced it, October 1835 by the first wooden house. And on this ground, in 1836 he erected the large adobe building known as Casa Grande."

Portsmouth Square (149), between Washington and Clay streets a block below Grant Avenue, is the place where the City of San Francisco was born. It was a plaza in the dusty Mexican town then called Yerba Buena. In the summer of 1846 the sloop-of-war *Portsmouth*, part of the American Pacific Squadron, sailed into the cove at the foot of Clay Street. The *Portsmouth*'s captain, Commander John B. Montgomery, ordered the Stars and Stripes hoisted on the plaza flagstaff. Then, to the echoes of a 21-gun salute from the *Portsmouth*, Montgomery proclaimed California to be American

A wide walking bridge spans Kearny Street from Portsmouth Square to the **Chinese Culture Center (150)**, located on the third floor of the Chinatown Holiday Inn. This is an excellent facility with free cultural classes, culinary workshops, films, lectures, and a marvelous gallery for art exhibits. There is a small museum shop too, which sells hard-to-find authentic folk arts. We found this delightful place to be well worth a visit. Open 10 A.M. to 5:30 P.M.; closed Monday.

Chinatown ■ 47

A stroke of this Buddha's belly insures luck, long life, and happiness.

The Chinese had a set time of day to relax over a cup of tea long before the British ever tasted tea. There is a word for teatime in almost every language. Here in Chinatown the word is *tiffin* or *dim sum* (Chinese for "a dot on the heart"). The English enjoy tea with little cakes and toast and jelly, but in the Chinese community tea is accompanied by delicate rice flour dough dumplings, *har gow*, each graced with a red dot. These feather-light buns contain shrimp or chopped beef or pork. *Won ton* is another variety of *dim sum*, shaped like an Italian ravioli. *Bows*, small puffy snowball-shaped pastry buns, are filled with pork and shrimp or chicken. Simply marvelous. End your teatime with something sweet, *jeel yeen bow* or *year see bow*, which contain coconut and brown sugar, or almond cookies.

Visitors to Chinatown should remember that *dim sum* is a noontime tradition, not one observed in the late afternoon as is British high tea. Most Chinatown residents are as much coffee drinkers as they are tea drinkers. You'll find coffee houses in Chinatown too.

Chinese tea is a Chinatown taste treat. Every restaurant waiter automatically serves a steaming pot of oolong, red, jasmine, or chrysanthemum tea with your meal. But by itself, or with a snack, a fresh pot of Chinese tea has marvelous pick-up qualities. As you saunter through the streets you will encounter dozens of cafes where you can stop for a refreshing pot of tea. Most of the shops along these sidewalks also sell boxed portions of tea that make nice gifts.

The Chinese herb shops along Grant Avenue and on some side streets have always been a curiosity to Westerners. For most of us, the thought of eating dried seaweed, or drinking a cup of lizard tea, conjures up all kinds of distasteful thoughts. Yet the Chinese people have a centuries-old tradition of using herbs and other more exotic substances for medicinal needs. For example, certain deer antlers are highly recommended for clearing ailments of the throat. Another kind of deer antler is said to be a potent aphrodisiac. Singers and speakers also benefit from scrapings of antlers. For asthma sufferers, there is a tea made by soaking new-born mice for a few months; this is said to give complete relief. For those who continually feel cold and would

Chinatown offers a diversity of trinkets and treasures.

ventative for colds and seems to give users body strength. American ginseng is said to be the most soothing. All the Chinatown herb shops and most health food stores carry ginseng root. It is similar in taste to a carrot and is sold dry. Brew it into a tea, or chew a dime-size piece of it. Some Chinese swear by it and say, "It puts lead in your pencil." At least that's what they say at the **Superior Trading Company (151)**, 837 Washington Street, where a large clientele praises ginseng as an aphrodisiac. Open seven days a week 9:30 A.M. to 6:30 P.M.

like to have warmer blood, the herbalist might recommend the following brew: take one small portion of dried rattlesnake and soak it in fresh water for one week until pliable. Then mince and add to your favorite yogurt recipe. Good luck!

In recent years Westerners have discovered that some of these exotic teas and tonics do indeed seem to have restorative powers. Ginseng root, with a tradition dating back thousands of years, has gained increasing popularity. Oddly enough, some of the best ginseng is grown in America, mostly in northern Wisconsin, and exported to the Orient. Ginseng is primarily a pre-

Chinese New Year is the most important celebration in Chinatown. Depending on the date of the full moon, it can fall any time between January 20 and February 20. This ancient ritual is observed by the explosion of thousands of firecrackers. The sometimes ear-splitting pops are meant to frighten away any lurking evil spirits. On the last night of the two-week-long New Year observance there is a colorful parade featuring centipede dragons that wind their way down Grant Avenue running a gauntlet of exploding firecrackers to the delight of huge crowds.

When you hear a burst of firecrackers at any other time of year you know that people are either practicing for Chinese New Year or warding off negative spirits at the entry of someone's new home or business.

An evening stroll through the streets and alleys of Chinatown is a good time to catch some of its most marvelous sights. Chinatown comes alive after dark. The always full sidewalks become jammed after the sun goes down. The dragon-entwined Chinese-lantern lamp posts and the pagoda-roofed buildings with elaborately ornamented balconies add to the exotic visual display.

On Grant Avenue the **Sun Sing Theatre (152)** and the **Old Chinatown Telephone Exchange (153)**, are pagoda-design buildings that were part of the model "Oriental City" project that also included the buildings at the corner of California Street and Grant Avenue. The builder, Look Tin Eli, was one of the founders of the old China Mail Steamship Company and the **Bank of Canton (154)**, with a branch now housed in the pagoda structure at 743 Washington Street near Grant Avenue.

The 1100 block of Grant Avenue, with its variety of smells and sounds, is reminiscent of old China. The **Dupont Market (155)** and **On Sang Poultry Company (156)** are excellent fish, pork, and poultry markets that attract many San Francisco residents. Boxes of live crabs, fresh fish and shrimp, and cages of quacking ducks and clucking chickens are an interesting contrast to the gaudy topless clubs of Broadway just around the corner. Several vegetable dealers along this part of Grant Avenue offer excellent fruits at any season. Watch for fresh water chestnuts, lichee nuts, and ginger root. During the day the shops receive their merchandise in wooden packing crates. Many of the imports from the Orient arrive in cases made from rough teakwood. The shop owners empty the cases and leave them on the street curb. Within minutes the packing cases vanish to become pieces of furniture, moldings, or bookcases in San Francisco apartments.

The northern end of Chinatown once stopped at Broadway. Today the streets around upper Grant Avenue that were the domain of beatniks and hippies in the 1950's and '60's are an extension of Chinatown.

From here, you can continue walking north on Grant Avenue to Broadway and on into North Beach (see page 82), or you can walk back to Jackson Street and turn east to visit the Jackson Square area two blocks down the hill.

You can catch a cable car from Chinatown by walking up the hill (west). The first block after Grant Avenue is Stockton, a street with a number of Chinese variety shops and grocery stores.

Mee Mee Bakery (157), at 1328 Stockton, is a fortune cookie factory which supplies many Chinatown restaurants. You can order a special batch of fortune cookies with your own predictions or special messages included. Open daily 9 A.M. to 6 P.M.

The next block as you continue up the hill is Powell Street. Northbound cable cars stop at the corner of Powell and Jackson; the stop for southbound cars is one block south at Washington Street.

The Coachman (158), an interesting British restaurant at 1057 Powell near the corner of Washington, opened during the 1950's. The owner is a chef who practiced his culinary arts aboard a cruise vessel until he jumped ship in San Francisco. Nothing exotic, but the cheerful English bar atmosphere together with a menu that includes kidney pie, casseroles, and Bombay chutney has stood the test of time. Open daily 5 P.M. to 11 P.M.; dinner 6 to 10:15 P.M.

Jackson Street

The Cable Car Barn and Museum

From Powell Street northbound cable cars make a scary 90 degree left turn onto Jackson. The next stop is the **Cable Car Barn and Museum** (159) on Mason between Washington and Jackson.

The red-brick car barn, 1201 Mason, is the heart of cable car operations. Here a giant electric motor turns a set of wheels 30 feet in diameter which pull the system's cable through the streets of San Francisco. You are invited to inspect the 100-year-old facility from a balcony floor overlooking the whole operation. Both the

Powell-Mason and the Powell-Hyde cable car lines pass the car barn. Ask the conductor for a transfer when you first board, and stop at the car barn on your way north to Fisherman's Wharf or on your return south to the Market Street turntable. The history and workings of the cable cars are well illustrated and displayed here in models, photographs, and faithfully restored old cars. You will also find any number of cable car souvenirs, books, and maps. Open daily 10 A.M. to 6 P.M. Free admission.

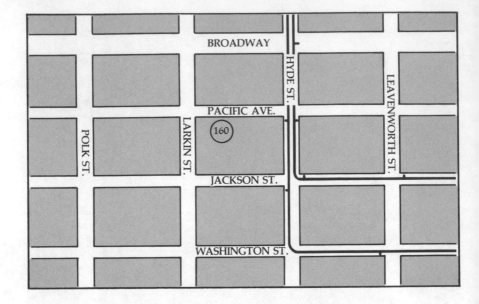

Essentially the cable car operation is simple. A continuous loop of wire rope is stretched between the power station and the turntables at both ends of each cable car line. Pulleys beneath the street, under the center slot, keep the swiftly moving cable in place. Keeping these pulleys in running order has caused the City much frustration. The cars themselves may work very well, but if the cable jumps the pulley, snags, or tears, a dozen other problems result. One day it will be necessary to shut down the whole operation and replace parts that were designed and built before the turn of the century. "Is it worth the expense?" is a question that has been raised; but most San Franciscans answer with a resounding "yes." We are very fond of the little streetcars, and it has been gratifying to see that people from all over the world care about them too. Donations are gratefully accepted by the Save the Cable Car Foundation, P.O. Box 2888, San Francisco, CA 94126.

Hyde Street

Russian Hill

From the Cable Car Barn and Museum on Mason Street, the Powell-Hyde cars climb up Jackson Street past Taylor, Jones, and Leavenworth streets to the corner of Hyde Street. Here the jaunty little cars turn right and parallel the spine of Russian Hill.

This area has been called Russian Hill since the 1820's when it was used as a burial ground for Russian soldiers and seal hunters who died from scurvy and other causes on their long sea voyage to the Golden Gate. At that time, only Catholics could be buried in the Mission Dolores cemetery, the area's only official graveyard. Non-Catholics had to be buried in the hills outside of Yerba Buena. So the Russians scaled the steep slopes and cliffs of Russian Hill to bury their dead in the claylike soil overlooking the Bay. The hill was used as a graveyard until the mid-1850's.

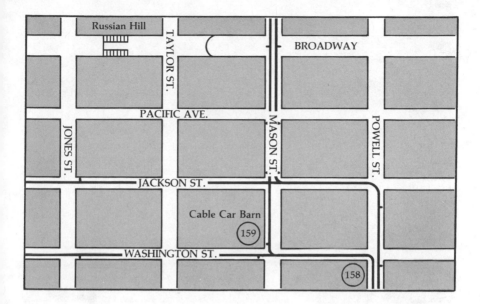

Another early name for Russian Hill was Hangman's Hill. It seems that at one time justice was carried out there from the branch of a tree.

Russian Hill began as a tourist attraction around 1870 when one of its first residents, Captain David Dobson, constructed an observatory platform at Lombard and Hyde and charged 25 cents for a look at his magnificent Bay view. Today the view is free.

About the same time, Comstock mining magnate George Hearst and his new bride, Phoebe, arrived in San Francisco on a steamer from the East Coast. As their ship passed through the Golden Gate, Phoebe pointed to Russian Hill and told her husband that those slopes would be the site of their new home. In two years their son, William Randolph Hearst, was born in the Stevenson Hotel on California and Montgomery streets. Soon after, the Hearst family moved into their new home at the southeast corner of Chestnut and Hyde.

The Hearst's move onto the Hill made the area a popular place to build large Victorian homes with elaborate gardens among the cypress trees. One of the residents was noted landscape architect Bruce Porter. His wife was the niece of Henry James and daughter of philosopher William James. Such names gave the area a reputation with local intellectuals. Soon more writers and artists found their way to Russian Hill, and it became the first bohemia in the fast-growing city.

Mark Twain and Bret Harte both lived in San Francisco during the 1860's. Twain worked on the *Call* newspaper as a reporter. He lived on Russian Hill, as did Frank Norris, Jack London, Gelett Burgess, George Sterling, John Dewey, Joaquin Miller, Will Irwin, Robert Louis Stevenson, and many other writers, photographers, and painters. The Hill is still the Montparnasse of the American West, but today most artists have moved farther east — down into North Beach or out to Potrero Hill to the south, or to Marin County.

The summit of Russian Hill offers a spectacular view of the City and Bay.

Dashiell Hammett, who set many of his legendary Sam Spade stories on the streets of San Francisco, lived on Russian Hill, at 1309 Hyde Street. He lived there with his wife, Josephine, and wrote his famed detective mysteries. Many of those yarns took place on Hyde Street. In the film version of Hammett's *Dark Passage,* Humphrey Bogart and Agnes Moorehead are seen fighting at a window, and the character played by Ms. Moorehead is pushed from the top story of the tall white apartment building at Hyde and Greenwich.

For avid Dashiell Hammett buffs there is a tour—the Dashiell Hammett Tour, led by local historian Don Herron. It begins in front of the Main San Francisco Public Library at McAllister and Larkin every Sunday at noon. This three-hour walking tour visits haunts of the legendary Sam Spade, and along the way Herron discusses Hammett's books in detail. The cost is $2, and it is best to confirm a reservation by calling Mr. Herron at 564-7021.

Few visitors consider these quiet residential blocks along Hyde Street worthy of much notice. But after you have been saturated with the hustle and bustle of Union Square, Chinatown, and Fisherman's Wharf, consider a leisurely stroll around Russian Hill to feel what it must be like to live at these heights. You might just leave your heart in San Francisco, as millions before you have done.

Just west of Hyde Street, on Pacific Avenue, is a place that's hard to resist. San Francisco is a sensuous city, a place to indulge yourself, and the ultimate indulgence for many San Franciscans is a piece of double-chocolate layer cake from **Just Desserts (160)**, at 1469 Pacific. If chocolate is not your desire, think of something you'd rather have; this enterprising group of people will probably have it. Crowded all day long, from 10:30 A.M. to 11 P.M.

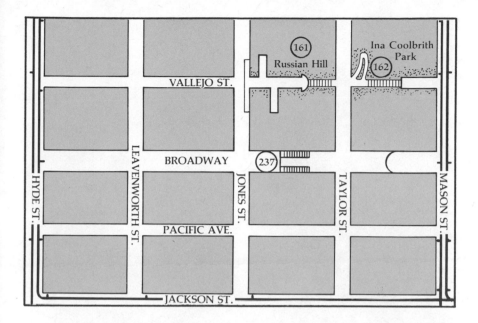

Vallejo Street

A walking tour of Russian Hill

To explore Russian Hill, you can take a fascinating walk along Vallejo Street above Jones, in a lovely, quiet residential area surrounded by marvelous vistas. The two narrow streets near the top of the hill, Russian Hill and Florence, are lined with brown-shingled homes, Japanese cherry trees, and well-tended gardens. These short streets branch off a cul-de-sac. On the lip of the hill, at a dead-end on Vallejo, is the **summit of Russian Hill (161)**. There is an unobstructed view of the Transamerica pyramid amidst a clutch of downtown financial district buildings; Treasure Island and the Bay Bridge lie beyond to the east. To the north are Fisherman's Wharf and the north bay region. At sundown, as the City lights go on, the views are unforgettable. From the top of this hill you can walk down a series of wide paths and steps that wind around well-cared-for shrubs and eucalyptus trees to Taylor Street

and the entrance to another green area, **Ina Coolbrith Park (162)**.

Ina Donna Coolbrith arrived in California on a wagon train from Illinois in 1852. She was the City's head librarian for 32 years and the first poet laureate of California. Local literary lights dedicated this acre in memory of Ina Coolbrith. Over the years residents and admirers have landscaped the property with trees and shrubs and a path that traverses the side of the hill. This is a peaceful place to sit for a time and enjoy the view of the City and a picnic lunch. Then continue down the wide paths to the next street, which is Mason; there you can pick up the Powell-Mason cable car, or walk on into North Beach for a cappuccino.

Lombard Street

The Crookedest Street

There is a cable car stop at Lombard and Hyde streets, the top of the "Crookedest Street in the World" (163). From here you can look east and see Telegraph Hill with Coit Tower at its peak. Once Telegraph Hill was the northern outskirts of San Francisco; later North Beach developed around the hill. Far in the distance, beyond the Berkeley hills across the Bay, is Mount Diablo, a long-dormant volcano named by Indians who believed that the devil himself dwelt deep inside the mountain.

In 1922 residents of the Lombard Street hill were summoned to City Hall. One Clyde Healy, a young engineer in the City Engineer's office, had a fascinating idea that could make access to Russian Hill a lot easier. Mr. Healy's suggestion was to reduce the steep slope from its 27-percent grade to a more manageable 16-percent by means of a system of hairpin turn-backs. It worked. For several years after the new street was built, there was two-way traffic on the Crookedest Street, but in time the City thought better of the idea and changed Lombard to the first one-way street in San Francisco.

Of course, the best photograph for the folks back home is a picture taken from the bottom of the Crookedest Street. You can walk straight down if you wish, but we suggest a little side trip that will give you a more intimate view of San Francisco. This slight detour will take you past the bottom of the Crookedest Street.

Begin this walk by getting off the cable car at Greenwich Street. On your left, up that brick street, is the **Alice Marble Tennis Courts (164)**. From that elevated vantage point you have a clear view of Coit Tower. In the far end of the block is a small park with views west; **George Sterling Park (165)** is dedicated to the poet whose home was nearby. Back across Hyde Street is a short extension of Greenwich Street ending in a cul-de-sac from which a wide stairway descends past several handsome homes to Leavenworth. Turn left on Leavenworth and you will find yourself a few steps away from Lombard, the Crookedest Street. From here you have several options:

1. You can climb back up Lombard to Hyde and catch the cable car to Fisherman's Wharf. 2. You can walk down the hill to the Powell-Mason cable car on Columbus Avenue. 3. You can continue your walking tour with a scenic stroll down to Fisherman's Wharf.

Follow Leavenworth up the ramp on the high side of the street as it curves around the hill; you will find a stairway to an elevated sidewalk that passes several stately homes and connects with Hyde Street. That green space across Hyde is the top of **Russian Hill Park (166)**. The fenced area is the roof of an abandoned reservoir. Between the tree line and the fence, to the right of the reservoir, is a wide dirt path with a panoramic view of the Bay all the way to the Golden Gate. Ghirardelli Square, which can be reached by a stairway at the west end of the park, is in the foreground.

The Hyde Street cable car climbs a 21-degree slope as it passes Francisco Street.

The view out toward the Pacific Ocean and the Golden Gate Bridge is spectacular. The controversial Colonel John Charles Fremont was a topographical engineer and explorer who was in California conducting a survey mission for the U.S. government. He wrote in his diary: "To this Gate I gave the name Chrysopylae, or Golden Gate, for the same reasons that the harbor of Byzantium was called, Chrysolceras, or Golden Horn."

For an even more incredible view, schedule a ride on the Hyde Street cable car just before sunset. There is nothing quite like the experience of sitting atop Russian Hill at one of the many marvelous vantage points and watching the sun set behind the Golden Gate Bridge. In the summer, the colors are diffused by fog rolling through the Gate. The smell of wood fires wafting up from shingled houses settles over the Hill and the City takes on a whole new mood. The cry of sea gulls heading in from the sea, the slapping of the cable under the tracks, the clanging of the cable car bells, and sometimes the foghorns—those unique sounds of San Francisco can best be experienced in the tranquil setting of Russian Hill.

As the lights come on, the waterfront takes on a fairyland quality. Have an Irish Coffee or dinner near the waterfront before returning over the Hill. There is something truly magical about rumbling home aboard the dimly lit cable car. As it slowly climbs the Hyde Street Hill and the piers recede behind you, look east toward Coit Tower. And watch for the sudden spectacular views of the Bay Bridge as you top the Hill. No wonder San Francisco is everyone's favorite City.

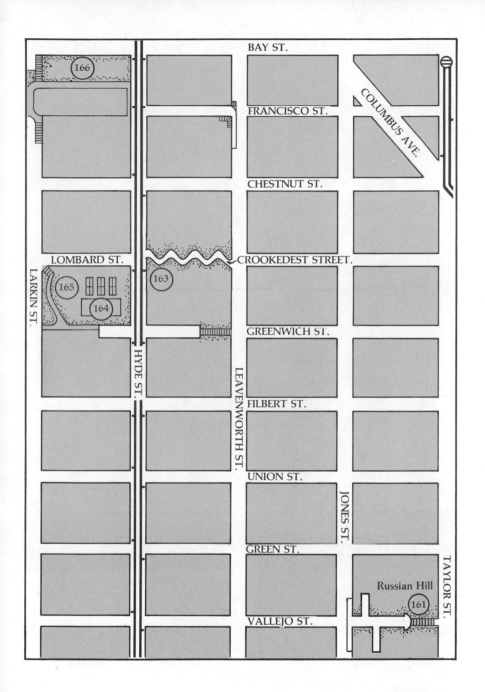

BAY ST.

FRANCISCO ST.

COLUMBUS AVE.

CHESTNUT ST.

LOMBARD ST.

CROOKEDEST STREET.

166

165

163

164

LARKIN ST.

HYDE ST.

LEAVENWORTH ST.

GREENWICH ST.

FILBERT ST.

UNION ST.

JONES ST.

GREEN ST.

Russian Hill

161

TAYLOR ST.

VALLEJO ST.

From the top of Hyde Street hill there is a breathtaking view of the Hyde Street Pier, Alcatraz and Angel islands, and the Bay.

FISHERMAN'S WHARF

Ghirardelli Square, The Maritime Museum and Hyde Street Pier, The Cannery, Pier 39, tour boats, museums, and amusements.

Here on the turntable in Victorian Park the cable car will be turned around to begin its return to Powell and Market. You can make your return on the same line, but more than likely you will want to wander along the Wharf and explore the unique shopping areas, restaurants, museums, and amusements. In that case, you can get back downtown on the Powell-Mason line from Bay and Taylor streets (see page 81).

Be sure to wear warm clothing for your trip to Fisherman's Wharf. Downtown weather might be sunny and warm, but near the waterfront the air can be cold and damp. And in summer and fall, the famous San Francisco fog rolls through the Golden Gate. San Franciscans will tell you that we have our winter in July.

San Franciscans are fond of the fog. It comes and goes like an interrupted love affair, fascinating and enchanting. The fog is formed when California's central valleys grow hot; the heated air rises and the cool marine air is pulled in to replace it. Cool air meeting the warm land forms the fog that you see pouring through the Gate, sometimes moving at a pace of 15 miles per hour. San Franciscans call the fog "natural air conditioning." Like the hills and the Bay and the cable cars, it is one of the City's cherished assets.

San Francisco's historic Fisherman's Wharf area starts at the bottom of Hyde Street hill, near the end of the cable car line.

Across from the cable car turntable is one of our favorite saloons, the **Buena Vista Cafe (167)**. Here you can enjoy an excellent old-fashioned breakfast or light luncheon. San Franciscans know this cafe as the "BV." It dates back to the 1870's. A famous San Francisco libation, Irish Coffee, was invented on the premises in the early 1950's. It is a delicious concoction of two parts hot coffee and one part Irish whiskey, with two sugar cubes and topped off with heavy cream.

In times past the rich aroma of chocolate drifted down the hill to the BV from a red brick factory on North Point Street. The spicy smell came from the D. Ghirardelli Company, manufacturers of chocolate since 1852. In those days you could also hear the shrill steam whistle that announced the beginning, middle, and end of the factory's workday.

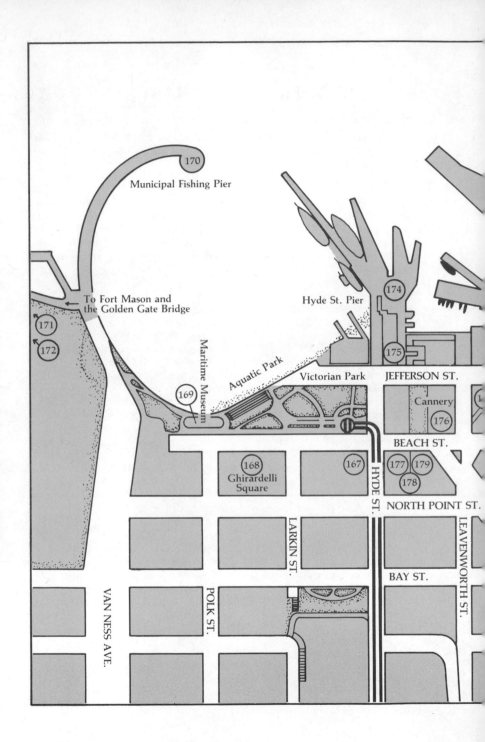

Municipal Fishing Pier

170

To Fort Mason and
the Golden Gate Bridge

171

172

Hyde St. Pier

174

175

Maritime Museum

Aquatic Park

Victorian Park

JEFFERSON ST.

169

Cannery

176

BEACH ST.

168

Ghirardelli
Square

167

177 179

178

HYDE ST.

NORTH POINT ST.

LARKIN ST.

VAN NESS AVE.

POLK ST.

BAY ST.

LEAVENWORTH ST.

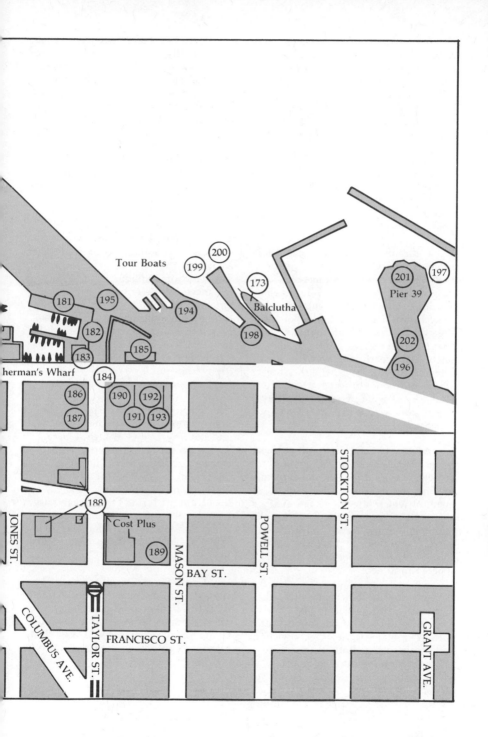

Tour Boats

Balclutha

Pier 39

herman's Wharf

Cost Plus

JONES ST.

TAYLOR ST.

COLUMBUS AVE.

FRANCISCO ST.

BAY ST.

MASON ST.

POWELL ST.

STOCKTON ST.

GRANT AVE.

Domingo Ghirardelli, a large square-faced man with a great bushy beard, came to San Francisco from Rapello, Italy by way of Peru. Ghirardelli slipped into town during the Gold Rush year of 1849 and headed straight for the gold fields. But he was no hunter of precious metal; three years later he found his fortune in a pot of chocolate. Toward the end of the 1880's Ghirardelli took over the factory works on North Point where the Heyneman-Pick Company had manufactured woolen uniforms and blankets for the Union Army during the Civil War.

Today these buildings house **Ghirardelli Square (168)**, a splendid complex of shops and restaurants. The main courtyard, built by Ghirardelli so that his employees could enjoy lunch away from the dust and grime of the street, is decorated with fountains and trees. It is an excellent place to sit, catch your breath, and do a bit of people watching. In general the shops are open Monday through Thursday 10:30 A.M. to 6 P.M.; Friday and Saturday 10:30 A.M. to 9 P.M.; Sunday 11 A.M. to 6 P.M.

At the information booth in the center of the plaza you can get a detailed map that locates and explains the Square's dozens of specialty shops, many of which offer items not available in other parts of the City. An old-fashioned saloon, terrace cafes with views of the Bay, bright flowers and shrubs enhance the leisurely atmosphere found here.

Try the **Via Veneto** for cocktails, light meals, or sandwiches and salads. Right next door is the **Portofino Caffe** with more majestic views, sandwiches, and exotic drinks. Both of these cafes are open Monday through Saturday 11 A.M. to midnight; Sunday 11 A.M. to 10 P.M.

A stone's throw away is the **Edelweiss**, a self-service restaurant offering its Swiss chef's delightful creations for breakfast, lunch, and evening snacks. Sit on the outside balcony and enjoy. Open daily from 9:30 A.M. to 5:30 P.M. Extended hours during the summer.

On the fourth floor of Ghirardelli Square is **The Mandarin,** "the finest all-around Chinese restaurant in the United States," according to restaurant critic Robert Finigan. Every year since it opened in June of 1968, The Mandarin has received the coveted Holiday Magazine Fine Dining Award. The fine Chinese cuisine ranges from traditional Mandarin to hot and spicy Szechwan. The handsome antique Chinese decor is enhanced by the original 1865 construction of red brick walls and wood-beamed building supports. The Mandarin's serene atmosphere and thoughtful service are extraordinary. Open Monday to Friday, noon to 11:30 P.M.; Saturday and Sunday 12:30 to 11:30 P.M. Reservations are advised; 673-8812.

Gift ideas can be perplexing for many people, so we are happy to suggest the possibilities at **Light Opera.** This shop specializes in art glass and Russian lacquer boxes. The boxes, painstakingly handcrafted and delicately painted, represent an increasingly rare art form. The Russian fairy tale scenes are our favorites. Open daily, Sunday through Thursday 10 A.M. to 6 P.M.; Friday and Saturday, 10 A.M. to 9 P.M.

Come Fly a Kite, at the Polk Street entrance to the Square, is stocked with beautiful multicolored paper kites, many from as far away as India and China. They make excellent wall decorations or gifts. And the bay front is a good place to fly a kite.

A visit to Ghirardelli Square would not be complete without a stop at the **Ghirardelli Chocolate Manufactory**. This old-fashioned soda fountain and candy shop is on the main plaza next to the east entrance of the complex. Try their "Strike It Rich" — marshmallow-covered mountains of chocolate ice cream, loaded with nuts and surrounded by Ghirardelli chocolate nuggets. Open Sunday through Thursday 11:30 A.M. to 10 P.M.; Friday and Saturday 11:30 A.M. to midnight. Summer hours: daily 11 A.M. to midnight.

The white three-story building across the street from Ghirardelli Square is the **National Maritime Museum (169)**. The building, which resembles a ship, was designed during the 1930's as a WPA project. The City fathers wanted to provide a public bathhouse and gardens for a frolicking, sunbathing public. Unfortunately the project planners did not consider the forces of nature. Aquatic Park seldom has the sort of weather that would

attract thousands of sun worshipers. But the building does make an excellent museum. The museum was the dream of its director, Karl Kortum, who also deserves credit for other important contributions to the Fisherman's Wharf area — Victorian Park, site of the cable car turntable, and the display of ships at Hyde Street Pier. His efforts also resulted in the acquisition of the sailing ship *Balclutha,* berthed at Pier 43.

Mr. Kortum has devoted years to the quest for important nautical artifacts, books, and manuscripts that present the whole maritime history of San Francisco. The museum's display of ship models and old photographs is truly remarkable. The collection also boasts a rare collection of whaling ship scrimshaw, several handsome sailing ship figureheads, rope "fancywork" (macrame), ship models in bottles, and

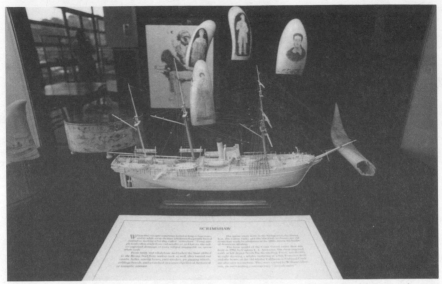

The National Maritime Museum is filled with nautical treasures: scrimshaw, ship models, figureheads, old photographs, and other memorabilia. This outstanding collection is open free to the public seven days a week.

dozens of other fascinating items of interest to anyone with a fondness for the sea. On an outside porch is a 19-foot wooden sloop that for 90 days was home to Kenichi Horie, a young sailor from Osaka, Japan. He was the first in modern times to sail alone 5,000 miles across the Pacific Ocean from the Orient to San Francisco. Open daily 10 A.M. to 5 P.M. The museum is free.

The **Municipal Pier (170),** which curves around in a crescent shape in front of the Maritime Museum, offers a splendid walk and a magnificent view of the Bay, Alcatraz Island, the Golden Gate Bridge, and the vessels going in and out of the Gate. During the sailing ship era the deep water in front of the Municipal Pier was the main San Francisco Bay deep-water anchorage.

From the Municipal Pier you can look west and see the piers that comprise the **Fort Mason Center (171).** That Liberty Ship is the *Jeremiah O'Brien,* one of the last remaining vessels from the Henry J. Kaiser Wonder Fleet of World War II. In the past these piers

and warehouses were a part of the huge San Francisco military port of embarcation. Now Fort Mason is part of the Golden Gate National Recreation Area—a huge park in San Francisco and Marin County, which includes a coastal strip around the City, from Fisherman's Wharf to the Golden Gate Bridge and continuing down the ocean shore. If you have time, and a good pair of walking shoes, take the Golden Gate Promenade—a three-mile path following the Bay, past Marina Green and the San Francisco Yacht Harbor, to Fort Point, under the Golden Gate Bridge. For maps or more information about the GGNRA, visit the park headquarters at Fort Mason, Building 201, or call 556-0560.

This grand old lady of the sea is built of steel and was used to haul grain and coal as well as cargos of whiskey and nitrate from Chile. During her last working years in the 1930's, the *Balclutha* served as a factory vessel on the Alaska run for the Oakland-based Star Fleet fishing enterprise. There is a small admission fee for the *Balclutha,* but a climb aboard this blue-water windbag is well worth the tariff. Below deck an exhibit traces the ship's years at sea. Open daily 9 A.M. to 11 P.M. Admission $2.00.

Also visible from the Municipal Pier are the historic ships displayed at the **Hyde Street Pier (174).** The pier, at the very foot of Hyde Street, once served as the ferryboat slip for the Berkeley and Sausalito White Fleet. Now it is part of the National Marine Museum and offers the public a fascinating look at West Coast seafaring history. The collection of ships includes the steam schooner *Wapama;* the three-masted schooner *C. A. Thayer;* the ocean-going tugboat *Hercules;* the *Alma,* a hay scow; and a survivor of the San Francisco Bay ferry fleet, *Eureka;* as well as several smaller craft.

These buildings at Fort Mason house a full spectrum of educational and cultural programs, and there are lawns, gardens, and picnic areas. There is also a vegetarian restaurant here: **Greens (172)** is open Tuesday through Saturday 11:30 A.M. to 2:30 P.M. Dinner on Fridays and Saturdays by reservation only; 771-6222. For a monthly calendar of classes, concerts, and other events at the Fort Mason Center, drop by the main office or call weekdays 441-5705.

Looking to the east along this northern shore you can see the three tall masts of the square-rigged sailing vessel, **Balclutha (173),** docked at Pier 43. The vessel is part of the National Maritime Museum and is one of the finest examples of America's great seafaring heritage. It is one of the famous old windjammers that made the hard trip from the East, around Cape Horn, to the West Coast.

The Hyde Street Pier is free and offers hours of adventure for sea lovers. A film entitled "The Last Voyage of the *C. A. Thayer*" is shown on board the ferryboat *Eureka.* It is only one of many excellent exhibits provided here. Young people will love the hand-held radio receivers provided at no charge to explain the various displays in the park.

Weekends at the Hyde Street Pier feature exhibitions of shipboard skills, lectures on nautical history, and programs of sea chantey singing. An annual Festival of the Sea is held during the last days of August. Open seven days a week 10 A.M. to 5 P.M.

Moored at the Hyde Street Pier is a collection of historic ships.

The sailors in the crowd will want to visit **Johnson & Joseph Company (175)**, one of the better-equipped ship chandlery stores in the Bay Area. This yacht equipment emporium sits next to the entrance to the Hyde Street Pier. It seems to have everything that goes on a boat—brass fittings, rope, sea charts, sea boots, foul- and fair-weather yachting clothes, a large selection of books and nautical souvenirs. Open every day 10 A.M. to 5:30 P.M.

The small wooden buildings along the beach near the pier are swimming and exercise clubs—the San Francisco Rowing Club, the South End Rowing Club, and the Dolphin Club. They were established in the 1870's. Their members are hearty souls, many of whom work out daily by taking a long swim in the Bay's 57-degree waters. Their route takes them out to the end of the Municipal Pier and back; look for their orange bathing caps bobbing through the water.

At the end of the first block of Jefferson Street is **The Cannery (176)**. The red brick building, which houses an even 50 boutiques, restaurants, and shops, looks like a tiny walled city with vaulted Roman windows and archways. Balconies look out onto a courtyard shaded by olive trees. Colorful pennants and flags create an old Italian atmosphere, and strolling musicians, jugglers, and clowns perform for your pleasure. Most of the shops and restaurants in The Cannery are open 10 A.M. to 10 P.M.

Before the turn of the century The Cannery was the old California Fruit Cannery. In the early 1960's a visionary Russian, who had changed his name to Leonard Martin, put up the money to convert the structure into an environment of shops and dining and entertainment establishments. There are hundreds of things to occupy your time at The Cannery. The work of designers and craftsmen is well displayed throughout. We found a store called **The Bath** that has bathroom items you would never think of. Rarely has a toilet seat been displayed in such an artful way, surrounded by a rainbow of towels, rugs, curtains, and perfumed lotions and soaps. Open seven days a week, 10 A.M. to 10 P.M.

In many of The Cannery shops you will find one-of-a-kind items that you will treasure for years to come. We found fashions with a continental casualness at **Barra of Italy.** The smell of leather drew us to **The Tannery** and its soft leather apparel and accessories. Nearby is a small shop called **The Mistress,** for the little nothings that one gives to one's amour. The shop has items of intimate apparel, the briefest sort of undergarments in hues, designs, and fabrics to make the heart palpitate. Lots to investigate here. Open 11:30 A.M.; closing time varies. And in The Cannery courtyard is an excellent pizza concession—**La Strada.**

The Nut Tree (177), at 655 Beach Street, across from The Cannery, has much to offer. The owner and his family started a highway fruit stand years ago near Vacaville, on the road to Sacramento. That family enterprise grew into a popular place for travelers to stop; today it even has its own fly-in facility for those who want to wing it. Bob Power, the family head, has a fondness for aircraft, Sir Francis Drake, and simple foods boldly displayed in a grand manner. In his Fisherman's Wharf gift shop, his first away from the family digs, he has gadgets and gifts and original art works, interspersed with tasty nut breads and poppy-seed cakes, homemade candy, and hand-painted cookies like those the family offered to highway travelers years ago. Open daily 10 A.M. to 10 P.M.

The Cannery courtyard.

Next door, the **Wine Museum (178)** has assembled a unique collection of wine history in the form of rare prints, photographs, drawings, sculptures, and decorative objects. The collection, compiled by the Christian Brothers Winery, includes the works of Picasso, Chagall, Daumier, and many other outstanding artists. It is all displayed in celebration of the grape. One of the most worthy attractions is the Franz Sichel glass collection, which spans 20 centuries and includes hundreds of etched crystal and engraved goblets. This is an excellent museum, and it's free. Museum hours: Tuesday through Saturday 11 A.M. to 5 P.M.; Sunday noon to 5 P.M.

At the corner of Columbus and Beach you'll find **North Beach Leathers (179).** Bill and Frank Morgan began their first leather shop here in North

There are numerous quiet recesses on Fisherman's Wharf where you can experience the sights, sounds, and smell of the sea. Pick out one for a secluded picnic.

Beach a dozen years ago. Today the brothers Morgan own a national chain of stores offering men and women the finest in leather, suede, and fur garments—expensive but with excellent value and design. Open 10 A.M. to 9 P.M.

Throughout San Francisco's history the City has had its street characters. One who works this part of Beach Street is Mr. Grimes Poznikov. He studied to be a teacher, but was caught up in the illegal weed and lost his right to professorship. Today Mr. Poznikov sits within the canvas walls of a 24-inch by 24-inch cell. He calls himself The Automatic Human Jukebox. "Just drop a coin in and get a tune." With the sound of a tribute being dropped into his tin can, Mr. Poznikov rolls up a section of canvas, his "curtain," and plays or sings a few bars of any request. He has been "established on Beach Street" since 1973.

The Anchorage (180), a recent addition to the building boom on Fisherman's Wharf, is on the next block of Beach Street. This structure houses a Howard Johnson's Motor Lodge with an entrance on Beach Street, and a shopping and restaurant complex with an entrance on Leavenworth.

At **Houlihan's** on the top floor of the Anchorage, you'll find a party atmosphere. This colorful San Francisco bar and restaurant offers a varied menu from hamburgers and sandwiches to steaks and seafood. The view of Jefferson Street and the rest of Fisherman's Wharf is intriguing. Moderately priced. Open from 11 A.M. to 11 P.M., with a Sunday brunch from 10:30 A.M. to 2 P.M. The bar and a disco are open until 1:30 A.M.

The heart of Fisherman's Wharf is the fishing fleet berthed for the most part between Jones and Taylor streets. During the 1950's, 2,500 men manned 1,000 fishing vessels docked at the wharf. Five hundred of those boats belonged to the crab fleet which begins its season in November and ends it in midsummer. Today the fleet is much smaller, but the crab fishermen still head out past the Golden Gate early in the dawn hours and return by midafternoon accompanied by hordes of screaming sea gulls.

Fish Road was an early name for Taylor Street. The general area was part of an old fish wharf where fishermen tied up their boats. It was here that the first crab cocktail was sold in a place called the Cobweb Palace. A bowl of clam or crab chowder cost five cents. The Cobweb Palace is gone now, and so are the nickel bowls of chowder; but the smell of the sea is still here, and so are the creaking sounds of wooden vessels chafing against the docks, and the cries of sea gulls.

Sportsmen who yearn for the roll of a wooden deck under their feet and the feel of a pole in their hands can take a sports fishing charter out for a day on the bounding main. The salmon season is from March to September, although there is bottom fishing year-around. The salmon boats require advance reservations. Most of the sports boats tied up along the docks are for hire. The best fishing is found a few miles beyond the headlands of the Golden Gate. The boats leave early, before daylight, treating you to the unique experience of watching the sunrise behind the Golden Gate Bridge.

The fishermen's Monterey-type boats are of a design that has been around for centuries. It was originated on the upper Nile during the Middle Ages and was used for generations in the Mediterranean before Sicilian fishermen brought the boats to Northern California. The boat hulls are between 28 and 36 feet long with a 12-foot beam. Today the Monterey-hull boats are powered by gasoline or diesel fuel; years ago these same boats were powered by the wind. Their sail plan was a triangular lateen sail which is still used to some degree today while at sea.

Every year in early September the fishing fleet is blessed at colorful ceremonies honoring Santa Maria del Lume (St. Mary of the Light), the patroness of fishermen. A procession begins at St. Peter and Paul's Church in North Beach, and ends with a ritual at Fisherman's Wharf. The fishermen pray for safe passage and bountiful fishing. Sailors are a conservative lot of God-fearing men who experience the power of their God every day they spend at sea.

Aside from the working boats, Fisherman's Wharf is a marvelous arcade devoted to seafood restaurants, many of which have sidewalk take-out counters, shops, art galleries, and many kinds of amusement. Names proudly emblazoned above busy restaurants in the area pay tribute to the Italian-American families who gave the Wharf its beginning and carry on the tradition today: Tarantino, Castagnola, Alioto, Sabella, Scoma. They represent just a few of the Italian-Americans who have achieved success in San Francisco's seafood industry.

What will it be? Filet of sole en papillote, sand dabs meuniere, abalone, crab cioppino? A long menu awaits you. The restaurants above street level have huge picture windows with handsome views of the Bay and the surrounding area. At the end of Taylor Street are several excellent choices for lunch or for dinner with views of the Golden Gate Bridge. **Fisherman's Grotto (181)**, **Alioto's (182)**, **Tarantino's (183)**, **A. Sabella's (184)**.

Perhaps a picnic is more your style. Those steaming caldrons in front of the restaurants are cooking up our famous West Coast Dungeness crab. The fishermen bring in these delicious crabs almost daily during the season. Choose a crab at any one of the many sidewalk stalls and have the man crack it for you. Then walk over to the **Boudin French Bread Shop (185)** at 156 Jefferson Street and pick up a loaf of the best sourdough bread in the City. You can also pick up a small bottle of wine or a salami sandwich on their famous French bread. Then head toward the water's edge. There is usually a place to sit on Pier 41. If you see people fishing on the docks, the docks are open. Another good place to have a picnic is on Pier 47 in back of Scoma's, at the foot of Jones Street. It's quiet, with just the sea gulls eagerly awaiting

A ride on the Bay will yield spectacular views of the City's skyline.

your leftovers. You may prefer to sit in the sand at Aquatic Park in front of the Maritime Museum, or to walk out onto the Municipal Pier. There are so many spots where you can find a short respite from the crowds.

If your feet begin getting tired and you want to return to your hotel, the Powell-Mason line is just three blocks up Taylor Street at Bay. Or here's a better way to rest your feet—why not hail one of the bicycle rickshaws? The driver will be happy to give you a tour —as long as you don't ask to go uphill.

As you proceed up Taylor toward the cable car you'll find more places of interest. This whole wharf area is replete with gift shops, boutiques, T-shirt shops, pizza and clam chowder cafes, all manner of places with items too numerous to mention. (But as you get farther from the sight of the boats and the water the magic begins to fade.)

For those craving a good old hamburger, watch for the golden arches right along your route. **McDonald's (186)**, at 2739 Taylor, is open seven days a week. Open Monday through Thursday 7 A.M. to 9:30 P.M.; Friday and Saturday till 11 P.M.; Sunday till 10 P.M. Another well-known hamburger shop, **Carl's Jr. (187)**, has an outlet at 2740 Taylor. Open Sunday through Thursday 10 A.M. to 9 P.M.; Friday and Saturday till 10 P.M.

Street entertainment abounds along many of the sidewalks at Fisherman's Wharf. Wherever you go, a musician or clown, a human jukebox, a mime, or a family of precision dancers is there to entertain you. Sidewalk artisans can be found in generous numbers around the Wharf area, particularly along Taylor Street. They display their work with great pride. You can find unique handicrafts in metal, wood, leather, and other materials.

Many sidewalk artisans offer their crafts along the avenues near the wharf.

Leave time to browse through **Cost Plus (188)**, before you board the cable car. During the late 1950's several teachers from San Francisco State College huddled together and came up with an interesting marketing concept. Their combined energies have blossomed into a large chain of retail stores. The original store was an empty warehouse that sold imported items from around the world at exceptionally low prices— wine from South America, fabrics from Japan, brass items from India, furniture from Hong Kong. Today the original Cost Plus has spread into three other buildings clustered around the corner near North Point, and the chain boasts over a dozen stores around the Bay Area. Several more Cost Plus outlets will open soon in other states. The main concept is bargains galore sold in a warehouse atmosphere. The large variety of merchandise is displayed in barrels and crates that appear to be just off the docks. There is some-

thing very attractive about the smell of teak and oakum. It makes you sense the presence of wharfside piers and ships from far-off lands. These clever people have marketed a waterfront warehouse experience. Open weekdays 10 A.M. to 9 P.M.; Saturday and Sunday 10 A.M. to 7 P.M.

Veneto's (189), 389 Bay, near the Powell-Mason cable car turntable, is a charming, romantic Venetian restaurant which includes an authentic gondola afloat on an actual canal. The owners perform selections from Italian opera and musical comedy on weekends. This attractive spot has been serving excellent seafood, pasta, and steaks for over half a century. Open Tuesday through Friday, 11:30 A.M. to 11 P.M.; Saturday and Sunday, dinner only.

The Balclutha, *docked at Pier 43, is one of the last remaining full-rigged Cape Horn windwagons. It is open to all the old salts-of-the-earth.*

For those with strong feet and a desire to continue exploring the Wharf, Jefferson Street between Taylor and Mason offers an array of amusement arcades.

Ripley's Believe It Or Not Museum (190), at 175 Jefferson, carries on a legend. The museum is the work of a former San Franciscan, Robert Leroy Ripley, who started collecting bizarre facts and objects when he was still a teenager. This famous museum houses 500 exhibits with over 2,000 oddities, which the whole family will enjoy — but might not necessarily believe. Open 10 A.M. to 10 P.M. Sunday through Thursday and till 12 P.M. on Friday and Saturday nights. Admission is $4.00 for adults and $2.00 for children under 12.

The **Wax Museum (191),** 145 Jefferson, is said to be America's largest and finest wax museum. Three floors of exhibits feature a Tomb of Tutankhamun, a Movie Stars Hall of Fame, a Hall of Heroes, even a chilling Chamber of Horrors. In all, there are over 275 life-size wax figures, all dressed in magnificent costumes. Open 10 A.M. to 10 P.M. Sunday through Thursday and till 11:30 on Friday and Saturday nights. Admission is $4.50 for adults and $2.00 for children 6 to 12 years old (children under 6 years old are admitted free).

Next door is the **Haunted Gold Mine (192)**, a West Coast version of the old fun house with a hall of mirrors, friendly ghosts, and other sophisticated illusions sure to delight the children. Open the same hours as the Wax Museum; admission for adults is $2.50 and $1.25 for children 6 to 12 years old.

Finally there is the **Enchanted World of Old San Francisco (193)**, an adventure ride in vintage cable cars which recreates a tour of San Francisco during the old days. Open the same hours as the Wax Museum; admission for adults is $2.00 and $1.00 for children 6 to 12 years old.

Now, how about taking a Bay tour aboard one of the modern smooth-riding triple-decked sightseeing vessels tied up nearby? The little ships depart from Pier 45, Pier 43½, or Pier 39 throughout the day. No matter what the weather, if the boats are able to go out, you can be sure of a wonderful experience. And when the weather is cooperating, the sunset tour is breathtaking. Remember that the Bay can get chilly — dress accordingly.

The sightseeing vessels take passengers out past Fort Mason along the Marina district, past the Palace of Fine Arts, site of the 1915 World's Fair, and under the Golden Gate Bridge near Fort Point. When the boats return they pass close to Alcatraz Island, then swing down past the docks for a wonderful view of the Ferry Building and the City skyline before returning to the Wharf area. The tour guides are well informed and trace a lot of history. The Red & White lines **Bay Cruise (194)**, which leaves from Pier 43½, takes approximately one hour and 15 minutes. The fare is $6.00 for adults and $4.00 for children 5 to 11 years old. 546-2810.

The **Gold Coast Cruise (195)** from Pier 45 takes a two-hour tour of the principal points on the Bay. These glass-enclosed vessels also have open decks and a snack bar; they leave three times a day, during the summer season only. 775-9108.

The **Blue & Gold Fleet (196)** operates triple-decker sightseeing boats. The 75-minute tour leaves from the foot of

Pier 39. The fares are $5.00 for adults, $4.00 for senior citizens, and $3.00 for children 5 to 11 years old. On Friday nights a special two-hour cruise, which leaves at 6:30 P.M., includes cocktails, dancing, and free hors d'oeuvres. 781-7877.

Sailors rate San Francisco Bay among the best sailing in the world. **Sail Tours (197)**, at Pier 39, will provide a boat for a day, a weekend, or longer. Where you go and for how long is up to you. Sail single-handed or with a licensed skipper, in 30-foot to 40-foot sailing yachts. From one to six passengers, with a three-hour charter minimum. Sunset sails and sailing instruction are available. Open every day 10 A.M. to sunset. 781-0070.

Commodore Helicopters (198) at Pier 43 offers helicopter tours that cover much of the same route followed by the sightseeing vessels. Fares for a four-minute ride are $10.00 for adults, $5.00 for children ten and under. Longer tours can be arranged for any party of four.

Boat tours to Angel Island (199) north of Alcatraz are available at Pier 43. The island has an interesting history dating back to the summer of 1775 when Manuel Ayala camped there. His ship, the *San Carlos,* was the first vessel known to have passed through the Golden Gate. At the beginning of the twentieth century the Public Health Service had a quarantine station located on the island. During World War II Italian and German prisoners of war waited out the war there. For a while the island yielded a bit of silver; later it provided rock to build a military fort on Alcatraz and pine trees that were used as pier pilings along the San Francisco waterfront.

Today Angel Island is a state park, popular with boaters, hikers, and picnickers. You can take a ferry from either Fisherman's Wharf or Tiburon to Hospital Cove on the northern shore of the island. The round-trip fair is $4.50 for adults and $2.50 for children 5 to 11 years old. Call Gold Coast Cruises 775-9108 for their schedule of departures. You can also call Harbor Carriers, 546-2815. Park rangers offer a guided tour to explore the island's history. The complete walk along Perimeter Road takes two hours. The trail is rugged so don't attempt it without stout walking shoes.

Also at Pier 43 are tour boats to **Alcatraz Island (200)**, the infamous federal penitentiary which operated from the 1930's to the 1960's. What was once a terrible place has become a favorite tourist spot. It's so popular that you must make a tour reservation a week or more in advance: 546-2805. Once in a while a group will cancel at the last minute, so you might get lucky and find a last-minute space on the boat going out to "the Rock." The round-trip fare is $2.50 for adults and $1.25 for children 5 to 11 years old.

During the Civil War Alcatraz Island was a fort, with ninety cannon protecting the Golden Gate. In 1934 the island became a prison. Al Capone was a prisoner on Alcatraz along with one of his associates, "Machine Gun" Kelly. Another prisoner was the "Bird Man of Alcatraz." Many inmates attempted to escape from Alcatraz, but none are officially known to have succeeded in their quest for freedom. There was no escape from the Rock.

One man working on Fisherman's Wharf knows Alcatraz literally inside and out. He is Clarence Carnes. For 30 years he called that cold rock home. Mr. Carnes paid his dues, and now you can find him in **The Rock Shop** at Pier 43. Open daily, 10 A.M. to 9 P.M.

Pier 39 (201) is a tribute to one man's dream. In the early 1970's restaurateur Warren Simmons walked past the broken-down remnants of pier sheds at the present site and happened to notice that the pier pilings were concrete. Simmons recognized the possibilities for using the still useful pilings, and that triggered an idea: to build his own dinner emporium out over the Bay waters. His wife reminded him that he would also have to build a pier to get there. The man finally got his pier, and then some.

Some of the original flavor of the docks in the old days lives on at Pier 39. **The Eagle Cafe (202)**, second deck in front, was literally picked up and moved to its present spot from its original location on the Embarcadero at the corner of Powell. The old wharf rats still come here for a great feed and a good bar. Nothing has changed inside. Breakfast is still the best. Homemade corned beef hash is a well-known specialty of the house, known, in fact, over the seven seas. So is the meat loaf. For coffee, you serve yourself. Open early and closed early.

Pier 39 offers Italian specialty restaurants, seafood and Mexican restaurants, fast-food stops, a wide range of gift shops, an espresso bar, sea treasures, book shops, a large western wear shop, poster shops, several places to taste California wines, a shop that specializes in cutouts and prints of Victorian houses, a miniature shop, and clothing stores. Visit the

Pier 39—the waterfront's new shopping, dining, and entertainment complex.

pier's nut shops, chocolate shops, pipe shops, shell shops. There's entertainment most of the time, and even a merry-go-round with a game arcade and a UFO exhibit. Over a hundred places to eat, shop, and have some fun. In general shops are open from 10:30 A.M. to 8:30 P.M. seven days a week; restaurants are open 11:30 A.M. to 11:30 P.M.

To get back to the downtown area from Pier 39 you have several options. The most popular, of course, is to take the Powell-Mason cable car from Bay and Taylor streets. If you want to avoid the crowds at the end of the day, get out your Muni map and check the several bus routes available to you. The #32 bus runs down Beach Street and along the Embarcadero. You can get off at the Ferry Building; walk across the Plaza to catch a bus up Market Street or the California Street cable car. The #39 Coit bus will take you from Beach and Powell streets to Coit Tower. If you get off at Washington Square you can transfer to the #30 bus which will take you past Union Square and Market Street. There is also the #15 bus from North Point and Taylor which runs through the Financial District and crosses Market Street at First Street. Don't forget to ask the driver for your transfer as you board the bus.

THE POWELL-MASON STREET LINE

#59 From Bay and Taylor streets
to Powell and Market streets

The #59 Powell-Mason cable car line's last stop is at Bay and Taylor streets. The turntable is three blocks south of the wharf. From this point the cable car returns downtown after skirting the edges of North Beach (San Francisco's Little Italy), Broadway, with its raucous nightclubs, and Chinatown.

Columbus Avenue

From the Wharf to North Beach

As the cable car leaves Taylor Street it swings up Columbus Avenue, a main artery to the downtown financial center.

At **The Boarding House (203)**, 901 Columbus, some of the best entertainment personalities in the country perform regularly. For over a decade this club has been presenting headliners in comedy and in pop, rock, and country music. Comics Steve Martin and Robin Williams were "discovered" at the Boarding House. Now aspiring entertainers have a venue in the basement room, Allen's Alley, named after comic Fred Allen. Showtime nightly at 8 and 11 P.M., Sunday 5 and 8 P.M. Minors are welcome. Call 441-4334 for reservations.

Out-of-town photographers will be happy to know that there is a photo lab available on an hourly basis at **Columbus Camera & Superlab (204)**, at 755 Columbus. The basement black-and-white darkroom facility has most of the equipment you need for developing film and making your own prints. Other photo services are also offered. The photo darkroom is limited to eight people working at one time, so it's best to make a reservation: 989-4004.

A century-old ritual is performed at the end of the line as the conductor and gripman push the cable car around the turntable to begin their trip back downtown.

North Beach

Filbert Street to Broadway

When you hop off the #59 Powell-Mason cable car at Union Street, walk downhill; at the foot of the hill is a unique oasis.

Washington Square (205), a grassy park on Columbus between Union and Filbert, is a good setting in which to relax. The ambience of this part of San Francisco is that of a neighborhood— quite a contrast to the bustling financial district and the carnival atmosphere of Fisherman's Wharf.

This square block of green lawns and poplar trees is the central plaza of North Beach, the general area in the

Facing the west side of Washington Square is the **Washington Square Bar and Grill (206)**, at 1707 Powell. This is an old-timer's place that is now very popular with the local writers and publishers, the media and other celebrities, as well as singles. Excellent is the word that describes the service and the Italian food. The menu changes daily, but standards such as minestrone soup with French sourdough bread will long be remembered. We recommend the baked salmon with shrimp sauce over rice, or the calamari with anchovies. An old-time saloon piano player provides music, and on weekend nights Dixieland jazz is featured. Open from 11:30 A.M. to 2 A.M.; reservations are a good idea: 982-8123.

Next door on the corner is **Beethoven Restaurant (207)**, a low-profile German restaurant. Dinners of *Bauernschmaus unt geschnezeltes kalbfleisch,* from 5:30 P.M. to 1:30 A.M. Very German and people love it; you should make reservations: 391-4488.

On the opposite corner is the **Powell Street Bar and Grill (208)**. This is an interesting bar that is more midwestern than San Franciscan. It's another Irishman's home away from home, and you generally find Ed Moose, the owner of the Washington Square Bar and Grill, here. Open 10:30 A.M. to late: 434-2150.

The Great Freeze (209), at 655 Union, is the place to go if you are in the mood for Bud's ice cream. Bud's is a high-butterfat confection that is legendary around town. One scoop of bittersweet chocolate on a cone will ruin a diet, but then how else will you know what you are missing? Sandwiches and other goodies-to-go; all you need for a picnic in the park. Open 10 A.M. to 8:30 P.M.

valley between the slopes of Russian Hill and Telegraph Hill. Almost every weekend and holiday is an occasion to set up a fair or some type of entertainment in Washington Square. No matter what direction you walk from this park, you are sure to find some adventure. North Beach is a favorite with all San Franciscans. So take along your camera and put on your walking shoes.

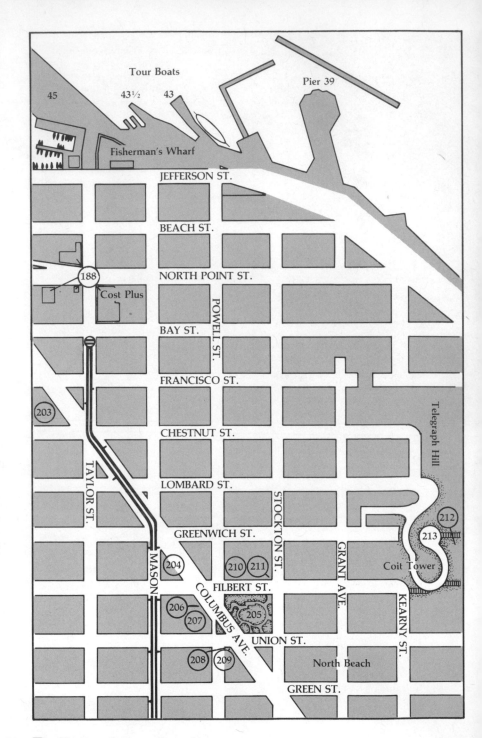

Julius Castle, perched atop Telegraph Hill, commands a breathtaking Bay view.

The #39 bus to Coit Tower stops in front of the Great Freeze. From the Tower it returns to Washington Square and continues on to Fisherman's Wharf. On the south side of Union Street at Washington Square you can catch a #41 bus across Union Street to the Victorian shops west of Van Ness Avenue.

One of the most attractive church buildings in the West is **St. Peter and Paul's Church (210)** on the north side of Washington Square. The twin towers of the church rise up tall and magnificent against the City's skyline. During the spring and on Columbus Day a parade of City politicians and young people begin a march here for the blessing of the fishing fleet at Fisherman's Wharf. The Italian weddings held here are generally lavish affairs, worthy of Hollywood.

Mama's (211), on the corner across the park at Filbert and Stockton, is a small restaurant that was established during the mid-60's as a breakfast and lunch cafe. The delicious omelets, homemade breads and pastries, as well as the attention given to the tasty fresh salads, quickly made this place a success. Two other Mama's can be found in town, on Nob Hill and at Macy's. Open from 8 A.M. to 8 P.M. every day.

If you care to make the climb to Coit Tower, continue walking up Filbert Street two steep blocks to the end. At the top of the hill you will find wooden steps that lead up toward the Tower. These are the Filbert Steps West. For many years these steps were the only means for occupants of the hill to get home. A second series of steps, the Greenwich Steps, can be

At the top of Coit Tower is an observation area, open seven days a week.

found one block north. These stairs emerge next to Coit Tower, and then descend to Montgomery Street and on to Sansome Street at the bottom of the Embarcadero side of Telegraph Hill. Midway down this long stairway is **Julius Castle (212)**, 302 Greenwich Street. This restaurant clings to the side of Telegraph Hill and has a sweeping view of the Bay. Open 5:30 A.M. to 9:45 P.M. Reservations required: 362-3042.

The view east, across the Bay, is of Yerba Buena Island; the flat fill area to the north side is Treasure Island, the site of the 1939 Golden Gate International Exposition. Now it's a Navy and Coast Guard facility. The San Francisco–Oakland Bay Bridge crosses over to the city of Oakland and the rest of the East Bay including Berkeley and Richmond.

During the early days of the City, Telegraph Hill was called Prospect Hill, then Signal Hill. The Spanish called it Loma Vista. The hill was important because from its top one had a clear view to the open sea, giving advance warning of inbound ships. A system of semaphore communications, erected by the crew of the *Portsmouth*, told the town the type of vessel coming into the Bay as much as two or three hours before the splash of its anchor in the cove below the hill, at the foot of Clay Street. A ship's arrival could mean party time and meeting new and old friends. It also meant mail and much needed supplies from the civilized Atlantic coast.

The first residents of the hill were gold seekers from South America on their way to the Sierra foothills. Soon enough the hill was known as the "Latin Quarter." Later the Irish established themselves there, then the Italians moved in. Today the expansion of Chinatown is diminishing the strong Italian influence in North Beach.

Coit Tower (213), atop Telegraph Hill, was the expression of a young woman's gratitude and affection for the City's hard-working fire fighters. During the 1890's, one of the more entertaining activities for young and old alike was watching the fire wagons race to a fire. In those days, a team of men or horses towed the water wagons to the frequent fires. When the wagons had to ascend the steep hills of the City, all able-bodied citizens gave a hand. There was even a competition between fire companies. The faster a pump-and-ladder company could respond to a fire, the larger the Christmas package from the thankful citizens. Each fire company also had its own adoring fans. One particular fan of the San Francisco Knickerbocker Fire Company Number Five was Lily Hitchcock. The daughter of a distinguished physician in town, Lily was a spirited young woman who liked to run after the fire wagons. One summer afternoon Lily responded to the ringing of the fire bell and caught up with her heroes, the Knickerbocker Number Five, huffing and puffing up Telegraph Hill. The steep slope had almost forced the fire wagon to a stop when Lily rushed into the road and began pushing one of the wagon's great spoke wheels. At the same time she screamed to passersby on the hill, "Come on, give a hand for Number Five!" The fire fighters of the Knickerbocker Number Five never forgot Lily's loyalty. They gave her a hat, a badge, and a stickpin with fourteen diamonds in the shape of a number five.

Lily later married Howard Coit. When she died she left some money to build a monument to the fire fighters of San Francisco. Most of the funds were used to construct Coit Tower, which was designed by architect Arthur Brown. The rest of Lily's money was spent for a bronze statue depicting her

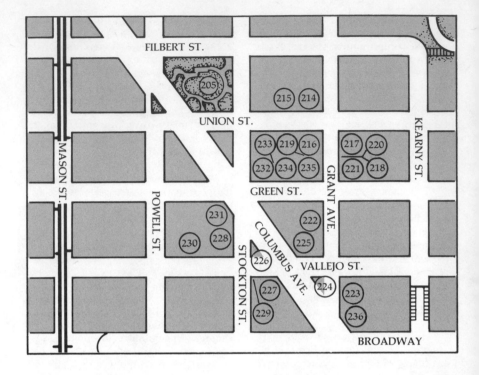

courageous fire-fighting heroes; it now resides in Washington Square Park, in North Beach.

One of the daily rituals for many people around North Beach is a stop in one of the scores of espresso cafes to enjoy a strong Italian coffee. **Malvina's (214)**, at 512 Union, is a cafe with plenty of morning light to help start the day. Malvina's and most of the cafes of North Beach roast their own secret blends of coffee beans daily. They also sell coffee beans as well as a number of coffee-making machines and supplies. Open daily 8 A.M. to 6 P.M., Sunday 9:30 A.M. to 5:30 P.M.

Above Malvina's is the **Museo Italo Americano** with changing exhibits of archeological and art treasures, as well as the works of contemporary Italian painters. Open Wednesday to Sunday from noon to 4 P.M.

Next door, at 524 Union, is **Cadell Place (215)**, a small jazz club that carries on a long tradition of bringing jazz and other types of music to North Beach. Open 4 P.M. to 2 A.M.; closed Monday.

On the corner of Grant Avenue and Union is **La Veranda (216)**, a small pizza place that also makes delicious cappuccino for the late afternoon crowd. Open 4 P.M. to 2 A.M.

This end of Grant Avenue maintains the strong ethnic feeling that attracts people to North Beach. Many of the shops have been here since the 1906 earthquake and fire. These days older beatniks, hippies, young punk rockers, and rough riders are all at home in the same clubs that were popular 30 and 40 and more years ago.

Cafe Jacqueline (217), at 1454 Grant, is a delightful small restaurant that will remind you of the Left Bank in Paris. The specialties are souffles: Gruyere, garlic, fresh spinach, prosciutto, and many others. During the 1950's this was called The Place, a hangout for beatniks. Open for lunch, Wednesday to Saturday from 11 A.M. to 2 P.M.; Sunday brunch 10 A.M. to 3 P.M.; closed Monday and Tuesday.

If you are looking for an old WW I German helmet, or an ivory-headed walking cane, or perhaps a mustache cup, or maybe an old Cola-Cola glass, or aviator goggles, **The Shlock Shop (218)**, at 1418 Grant Avenue, will have it and a thousand other odd discards that are now collectibles. This shop has been here for over twenty-five years. Open 10:30 A.M. to 7:30 P.M.

Mexican food, anyone? San Francisco has many small Mexican restaurants. **Casa Cortes Taqueria (219)**, at 1441 Grant, keeps up the international reputation of this street. Open Sunday to Thursday from 11:30 A.M. to midnight, and Friday and Saturday from noon to 2 A.M.

We found an intriguing clothing shop at 1424 Grant Avenue called **Kyriakos of Hydra (220)**. Lots of loose-fitting clothes, some excellent wool sweaters, and jewelry, mostly from Greece. Open 10 A.M. to 9 P.M.

East/West Leather (221), at 1400 Grant Avenue on the corner of Grant and Green, has an extensive offering of leather jackets for men and women, nice leather shirts, and Frye boots. The prices are moderate compared to other shops selling leather garments. Open seven days a week 9:30 A.M. to 8:30 P.M.

Down on the next block is an old hardware store that hasn't changed since 1907. If you want to take a glimpse into the past, step into **Figoni Hardware (222)**, at 1351 Grant Avenue.

A North Beach claim to fame is the excellent selection of Italian bakeries.

The Caffe Roma, or a dozen similar cafes, serves excellent cappuccino and espresso.

There are several establishments in North Beach that haven't changed since before the turn of the century.

Such a place is **The Saloon (223)**, a well-aged watering hole at 1232 Grant Avenue next to Fresno Alley. Step inside the old swinging doors to San Francisco of 1861. You'll hear loud strains of opera music, singing customers, shouts and laughter, and the occasional barking dog. Nothing much has been altered in more than a century of existence. This saloon is a bit frayed at the edges, but marvelous. Open noon to 2 A.M.

One of our regular stops in North Beach is **Caffe Trieste (224)**, at the corner of Vallejo and Grant Avenue. During most Saturday mornings this cafe becomes the setting of an Italian opera; local mandolin and accordian players, as well as opera singers (including owner Johnny Giotta and family) come here to perform. We are especially fond of the Trieste's secret blends of espresso and their offering of pastries from the Victoria Bakery. Open from 7 A.M. to 11 P.M. Monday through Saturday; Sunday from 7 A.M. to 10 P.M.

Around the corner, at 414 Columbus, is **Caffe Roma (225)**, with a different view but with the same old-world atmosphere found at the Trieste. The walls and the ceiling are covered with classical murals, but the show is really the people seated around you. The person sharing your table could be poet Lawrence Ferlinghetti, author Herb Gold, artist Satty, or a local shop keeper. The crowds at both of these coffee houses can get heavy during weekends, so don't be timid about walking in, picking up your cappuccino at the bar, and staking out a seat. Open seven days a week 8 A.M. to midnight.

their other mouth-watering Italian foods. The Molinari brothers will make up sandwiches for you to take out for a lunch on the green. Open 9 A.M. to 6 P.M.

Another choice deli of the same vintage is **Panelli Brothers Delicatessen (228)**, at 1419 Stockton. Between these two establishments you can find still more delicatessens displaying mounds of meats and olives, wheels of cheese, hanging salamis, and a whole range of Italian taste treats. Open Monday through Saturday 8 A.M. to 5 P.M.

In North Beach our preferred Italian bakery is the **Victoria Pastry Company (229)**, on the corner of Stockton and Vallejo. Many of the cafes in this area purchase their bakery items here. There's one thing you should know: the best pastries are usually gone by noon. Open 8 A.M. to 5 P.M.

Across the street, on the corner, is the **Postermart (226)**. This is Ben Freedman's second poster store since the mid-60's when his shop was the first to sell Fillmore Auditorium posters. Reprints of the old Fillmore posters are still available at Ben's, along with thousands of new posters from around the world. The large feline that dominates the counter top answers to the name of Kitty. Open about 11 A.M. to about 11 P.M. every day.

On the opposite corner, at Vallejo and Columbus, you will find one of the neighborhood's earliest delicatessens, **Molinari's (227)**. This marvelous deli first started business during the 1890's, and the rich aroma that permeates the whole building reflects the decades of offering customers salami, prosciutto, garlicky galantines, olive oils, and all

During the 1950's the world knew this part of San Francisco as the beatnik capital, giving fame to Jack Kerouac, Kenneth Rexroth, Lawrence Ferlinghetti, Allen Ginsberg, and many other artists, poets, and writers. During the 1960's North Beach gave birth to topless entertainment and was a haven for displaced hippies from the Haight-Ashbury, on the other side of town. These days a few of the old clubs and hangouts are still in existence—many with new names and under new management—but the spirit and the characters are still around.

Years ago *the* jazz club in San Francisco was the Black Hawk. But for the past decade, since the Black Hawk was turned into a parking lot, the West Coast jazz scene radiates from the **Keystone Korner (230)**, at 750 Vallejo. The Keystone features such jazz greats as Stan Getz, Tito Puente, Milt Jackson, Shelly Manne, and even the jazz bands. There's a door charge and minimum. Open 8 P.M. to 2 A.M.; closed Monday.

The **North Beach Museum (231)**, on the second floor of the Eureka Federal Savings Bank at 1435 Stockton near the corner of Columbus, documents the ethnic development of North Beach. Exhibits feature incredible old photographs, articles of clothing, household items, toys, and miscellaneous artifacts, giving one a marvelous perspective of what this part of town was like a century ago. These outstanding exhibits change every four months. Open Monday through Friday, 9 A.M. to 4 P.M., Saturday 9 A.M. to 3 P.M.; free admission.

One of the many pleasant ingredients of North Beach life is the large number of family-style restaurants. You don't have to travel very far before encountering the delightful aroma of Italian or French cooking wafting across your path. Everyone who knows North Beach has his favorite. These tiny storefront restaurants serve food as delicious and unique as the larger dinner places. The choice of entrees is usually limited and sometimes chalked on a blackboard, but the food is always tasty with generous use of garlic, olive oil, fine herbs, and butter, and the atmosphere is congenial. The prices vary but average between $4 for lunch and $7.50 for dinner.

Green Street between Columbus and Grant avenues is typical of many North Beach side streets where you will find a spectrum of excellent Italian restaurants that have been in business for decades. From the intersection of Columbus and Stockton on Green you will locate a half dozen places where you can enjoy all manner of pizza, minestrone, pasta of every kind, scallopine, and other traditional Italian delights.

First on this sidewalk is the **Columbus Cafe (232)**, at 562 Green; next door is the century-old **New Pisa (233)**, at 550 Green; followed by a pizza shop, the **Golden Boy (234)**, at 542 Green; then the **Green Valley Restaurant (235)**, at 510 Green. These restaurants are open for lunch from 11:30 A.M. to 2 P.M., and dinner from 5 P.M. to 10 P.M.

At 1234 Grant Avenue is **La Pintera Cafe (236)**, an Italian family-style lunch and dinner restaurant which has been at this location since 1907. When the menu reads boiled beef they neglect to add that the beef is prepared with garlic, olive oil, parsley, and all the other ingredients native to the Tuscan region where the recipe was conceived. All the entrees are excellent. Open for lunch 11:30 A.M. to 2:30 P.M., dinner 5 P.M. to 11 P.M.

Along the 300 and 400 block of Columbus are still more small Italian restaurants. Names such as Guido, Luigi, Giotta, Puccini, and others have delighted their dinner customers for generations.

Broadway

The Entertainment Strip

The #59 Powell-Mason cable car rumbles to a stop above the Broadway Tunnel, the main artery through Russian Hill connecting Golden Gate Bridge traffic to the downtown financial district.

The intersection of Broadway and Mason Street is a good stop for a tour of North Beach's topless entertainment strip. By walking down the hill three blocks you will end up in the heart of it all. But first there is a marvelous place to take your camera for some stunning views of the City: the tree-shaded top of the **Broadway stairs (237)** looks out over the Bay, and weather permitting, you can see Mt. Diablo 40 miles to the east.

On your climb up the hill, you will pass **Our Lady of Guadalupe Church (238)**, at 980 Broadway, which is one of the older church buildings in the City. This handsome church was built in 1896, and its old Spanish design is typical of the California missions. The interior of this church is particularly impressive, with an ornate gold-leaf altar and exquisite stained-glass windows. Open every day from 7 A.M.; Sunday masses at 8, 9, and 10:15 A.M., with a Spanish mass at 12:15 P.M.

As you begin your descent down Broadway you'll see **Alfred's (239)**, at 886 Broadway, an Italian restaurant that boasts weekly shipments of Chicago beef. Besides choice selections of steak, Alfred's offers a whole range of Italian cookery. Open from 4 P.M. to 12:30 A.M.; closed Sunday.

Broadway, between Stockton and Montgomery, is San Francisco's midway of topless clubs. It has run the gamut of topless-bottomless live sex shows, "topless co-eds," "lady wrestlers," male strippers, female nude models, sex encounter clubs, female impersonators . . . the list is long. Every few months the club acts go from tame to vulgar, then the City vice cops make a sweep, and the owners clean up their acts until the next time.

The intersection of Broadway and Columbus is similar in many ways to New York's Times Square. The mainstream of San Francisco flows past these corners 24 hours a day.

When you look south down Columbus toward downtown San Francisco, you can see the **Transamerica Pyramid (240)**. The architects chose to depart from the traditional architectural maxim that form follows function, and thus gave fuel to those who opposed the building's construction in the late 1960's. The tip-top is 853 feet, 48 stories above the street, but the last 200 feet is an empty spire. These days most San Franciscans seem to be growing fond of this particular skyscraper. It has become a symbol of our City—a unique building for a unique town. Those two windowless protrusions, rising verti-

One of America's leading poets, Lawrence Ferlinghetti, established **City Lights Books Inc. (241)**, at 261 Columbus just south of Broadway, during the early 1950's. This small book shop has an extensive collection of poetry, theater, arts, and literature paperbacks as well as magazines devoted to these subjects. Writers and artists from around the world use City Lights as both a meeting ground and a facility for occasional readings. Open 10 A.M. to 11 P.M. every day.

Vesuvio Cafe (242), across the Adler Street alley from City Lights, is the creation of Henri Lenoir, an esteemed San Francisco bar owner. His North Beach way station has been the headquarters of writers, poets, and artists for decades. The Tiffany lamps and memorabilia create a Bohemian atmosphere where the greats and near-greats congregate, bend elbows, and trade gossip. Open early and closed late.

Now back on the corner of Broadway and Columbus is the City's first topless place, **The Condor Club (243)**. This club started in 1964 with Carol Doda being the first to bare all as a nightly feature that quickly captured the world's attention. Ms. Doda continues her act, a dance on top of a piano that descends from the club's ceiling at showtime. Open noon to 2 A.M.; $5 minimum.

cally from the midpoint, house the elevators. On the plaza level overlooking a tiny half-acre redwood park are the **Park Exchange Restaurant** and the **Park Exchange Bar.** Both these places have a Gold Rush saloon theme. At night the bar is turned into a disco and is open till the wee hours. If you care to have a picnic lunch in the park, you can pick up a carry-out sandwich from **Duncan's Delicatessen** on the plaza level. Open weekdays for lunch from 11 A.M. to 3 P.M. An observation room on the 27th floor is open Monday to Friday, 9 A.M. to 5 P.M.

For decades out-of-town folks have been flocking to **Finocchio's (244)**, upstairs at 506 Broadway. Finocchio means "fairy" in Italian, and the entertainment here is highly developed female impersonation: wigs, false bosoms, and laughs. Every evening the customers line up around the block to see this popular one-hour show. Showtime from 8 P.M. to 2 A.M.; closed Monday and Thursday; $4 admission; no minors allowed.

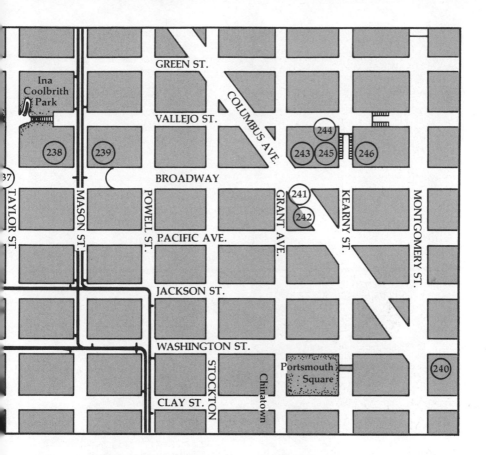

The ground-floor level of this address is a popular San Francisco mecca, **Enrico's (245)**. This is a successful sidewalk cafe which for many years has been a favorite of our town's celebrities cum entourage, and business people. People-watching while sipping a cappuccino is a tradition here. The rotund gentleman in the black beret is owner Enrico Banducci. Open seven days a week 11 A.M. to 3 A.M.

There is an extraordinary selection of excellent restaurants scattered among the topless joints. One of the best Italian restaurants in town is **Vanessi's (246)**, at 498 Broadway at Kearny. The bar and dining room is always filled with show business personalities and localites from the hill. Behind the main counter, the cooks working over their ovens and broilers present fascinating entertainment while you dine. The sight and aroma of steaks on the broiler, a cook preparing a cheese sauce, an order of scallopini, a baked lasagne, or a veal parmigiana is simply *fuera del mundo*. This marvelous mealtime show will make your visit to San Francisco memorable. Open 10 A.M. to 2 A.M.; closed Monday. Reservations are necessary: 421-0890.

THE CALIFORNIA STREET LINE

#61 — From Market Street at California and Drumm streets to Van Ness Avenue

The California Street line begins in the Financial District near the Ferry Building, crosses Chinatown's Grant Avenue, and continues up and over Nob Hill, passing the Stanford Court Hotel, the Fairmont Hotel, the Mark Hopkins Hotel, Grace Cathedral, several posh restaurants, and other places that will surely interest you. After passing over the top of the hill, the cable car drops down into Polk Gulch, then out to Van Ness Avenue, the end of the line.

On April 10, 1878, the California Cable Car Line, built by the enterprising Leland Stanford, commenced business with its first scheduled run out California Street. The line started at the corner of Market and Drumm streets near the present cable car stop. In 1878, it traveled up and over Nob Hill out into an expanse of sand hills that rolled like a desolate sea clear up to Twin Peaks. It was a barren wasteland that would quickly change into row upon row of Victorian houses.

The California Cable Car Line conductors were dubbed "the cavaliers of the turntables." Each morning the gripmen and conductors were inspected by Stanford himself to make sure that uniforms were in proper order: "silver buttons polished to a brilliant shine, mustaches well waxed, and a fresh baby rose pinned to the conductor's uniform lapel." The drivers were instructed to be chatty with passengers and to help elderly customers on and off the cars whenever possible. The City's other cable car conductors were held up in pale contrast to the gentlemen of the California Street #61 line.

The start of the California Street line is just a few blocks from the San Francisco waterfront. During its early days, San Francisco's waterfront was along Montgomery Street. The high-water mark looped around Telegraph Hill creating a cove at the foot of Clay Street. This was the cove where the sloop-of-war *Portsmouth* anchored in 1846. Thirty-six months and a gold rush later, over 600 vessels of every description jammed the cove, most of them abandoned by their gold-hungry crews. In the end the bones of those vessels became fill for the cove, parts of nearby Telegraph Hill, Union Square, and Market Street.

Before the Embarcadero received its Spanish name, it was called East Street. In its heyday it was a rough waterfront area crowded with the notorious crimps and shanghaiers, prostitutes and fun-seeking sailors who gave "Frisco town" its color in the 1890's. The old sailing vessel, *Balclutha*, berthed at Fisherman's Wharf, is the last reminder of the forest of masts and rigging that were once silhouetted against the Embarcadero's sky.

The historic Ferry Building now houses the World Trade Center and state offices, as well as the Division of Mines and Geology museum and library.

The Ferry Building

Ferries to Sausalito, Tiburon, and Larkspur

The handsome building with a clock tower on the Embarcadero is the San Francisco **Ferry Building (247).** In its day it was the second largest passenger terminal in the world (Charing Cross Station in London was first). The distinguishing clock tower is a symbol of San Francisco recognized around the world. The Ferry Building's north and south wings house state offices, the World Trade Center, and the San Francisco Port Authority. The California Division of Mines and Geology, in the southern wing, offers visitors rooms filled with dazzling displays of minerals, rock and ore specimens, and one of the finest reference libraries for mining, geology, and earth sciences. California county topographic maps and other useful information are available here, mostly free to the public. Open daily 8:00 A.M. to 4:30 P.M.; no admission charge.

Until the late 1930's great black and white, red, or green ferryboats, from a dozen different routes, arrived at or departed from the San Francisco ferry slips every three minutes with passengers bound for the fast-growing North and East Bay communities. (A survivor of the ferryboat fleet, the Northwestern Pacific Company's *Eureka,* is on public display at the Hyde Street Pier, Aquatic Park.)

Ferryboats leaving from the Ferry Building provide several Bay Area communities with links to San Francisco. The Red and White Fleet, which operates scheduled service to both Tiburon and Angel Island from Pier 43½ at Fisherman's Wharf, has service from the Ferry Building at peak commute hours. Phone 546-2815 for information.

The Golden Gate Ferry operates from the Ferry Building with service to Sausalito and Larkspur in Marin County. The Golden Gate Ferry information number is 332-6600.

You can start an interesting all-day tour of the Bay and Marin County by boarding a Golden Gate Ferry for Sausalito. Ask for a transfer before getting on. After you explore Sausalito, pick up a #10 transit bus. The bus will take you around Richardson Bay to the lovely bayside community of Tiburon. In Tiburon you can enjoy the magnificent waterfront, the unique shops, and lunch under an umbrella on the deck at Sam's or The Dock. Then proceed by ferry to Angel Island. From there, catch the ferry back to San Francisco. Needless to say, the views of San Francisco from the ferryboats are always marvelous.

Ferry boats depart from a new berthing facility behind the Ferry Building.

Embarcadero Center

Shops and restaurants

Before boarding the California Street cable car, you may want to explore the spectacular Embarcadero Center complex just west of the cable car terminal.

This series of high-rise buildings is a $300 million real estate project started during the 1960's by the Rockefeller family. In years past much of the area north of Market Street, around the waterfront, was the City's wholesale produce section. Today the **Hyatt Regency Hotel (248)** stands at one corner of the Rockefellers' ten-block project. Architect John Portman received numerous architectural awards for its design. The central lobby is a huge 17-story public atrium. It includes trees, fountains, and sculptures, and an assortment of restaurants and specialty shops. Public art exhibits are found throughout the hotel. Glass elevators rise past ivy-draped balconies to the City's only revolving rooftop restaurant and lounge, the **Equinox.** The view alone makes it very special. Lunch is served 11 A.M. till 3 P.M., dinner till 8:30 P.M. The hotel also has a sidewalk cafe, complete with umbrellas, on Market Street; it is called the **Market Terrace.**

On Sundays the Hyatt's **Atrium Lobby** is turned into a cafe-style dining room for brunch, 10 A.M. to 3:30 P.M. On Fridays, from 5:30 to 8:30 P.M., the atrium is filled with the sounds of Big Band music for tea dancing. Dancing is open to the public—no charge, no minimum; you can't beat it as a unique form of free entertainment.

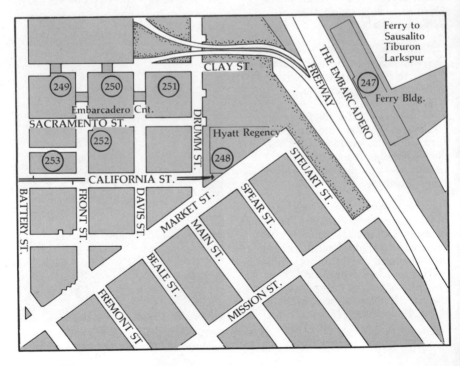

Restaurants and fine boutiques surround the Hyatt Regency atrium amid fountains, trees and sculpture, and glass-enclosed elevators.

Also included in the Embarcadero Center complex are the 45-story Security Pacific Bank building, **One Embarcadero Center (249)**; the 32-story Levi Strauss Building, **Two Embarcadero Center (250)**, with its history room exhibit of blue jeans that date back to the Gold Rush; and the 32-story building at **Three Embarcadero Center (251)**. These buildings are connected by a series of beautifully landscaped walkways and open air plazas featuring monumental sculptures. Here, in three levels above the street, you'll find an array of excellent restaurants, bars, boutiques, coffee houses, and cafes. At lunch time, the occupants of these tall buildings pour out to spend noontime on the promenades and in the nearby restaurants. You may prefer to avoid the lunch hour. Most shops are open Monday through Friday 10 A.M. to 6 P.M.; Saturday till 5 P.M.; closed Sunday.

As can be expected in this part of town, there is a variety of places to have a good lunch or dinner. At 240 Front Street is **Schroeder's (252)**, a German restaurant that is a long time favorite of generations of San Franciscans. The specialty of the house is sauerbraten with potato pancakes. Our preference is their delicious schweizer bratwurst with red cabbage. The dining room, furnished with round tables and a long bar, is as close as you can come to finding authentic German atmosphere in downtown San Francisco. Prices here are moderate and the food is always excellent. Open 11:30 A.M. to 9:30 P.M.

Tadich Grill (253), "The Original Cold Day Restaurant," is in the next block, at 240 California Street. The restaurant's reputation goes back to the Gold Rush days of 1849. San Franciscans love this excellent seafood place for its long menu and generous portions of fresh fish. The environment is simple and prices are moderate. You will see some people in evening clothes and others in informal street wear, sitting on swivel counter stools or in back booths, or waiting in long lines to get in. Dining here is an eating adventure well worth your time. Open daily except Sunday 11:30 A.M. to 8:30 P.M.

As the cable car rattles up California Street it passes an area that for many years has been referred to as the "California Street Yacht Club." This is where the City's business district started, with the foundations of most of the buildings literally resting on the bones of hundreds of ships. During 1849 vessels abandoned here by their gold-fevered crews served as shelter until the city could be built. Excavations in the area always unearth treasured artifacts from those early times. Today, this area is the domain of the West Coast's leading financial institutions—insurance companies, corporation headquarters, and banks.

The headquarters of many of America's oldest financial institutions are housed on lower California Street.

The Pacific Stock Exchange.

Sansome Street

The Financial District

Several of the major corporations in this downtown section have free exhibits, open to the public, which give a spark of life to this otherwise strictly business environment. Note that most are open only on weekdays, during regular business hours.

One block south of California Street, on the corner of Sansome and Pine streets, is the **Pacific Stock Exchange (254)**. For visitors who wish to watch the frantic pace on the trading floor, there is a gallery open to the public weekdays from 7:00 A.M. to 2:30 P.M. The entrance is at 155 Sansome Street, and it's free.

The dramatic history of oil is illustrated in an entertaining exhibit at the **Chevron Oil Building (255)**, 555 Market Street at Sansome. The World of Oil tour begins with a motion picture that explains the origins of oil. Attractive displays include photographs, tools, models of drilling rigs, refinery towers, and tanker vessels. Another series of exhibits traces the use of oil since the turn of the century. An early American kitchen and living room with full size figures, an early gas station, and a 1904 Ford automobile all illustrate how gasoline was used circa 1905. Guided tours are available. Open 9 A.M. to 4 P.M.; closed weekends and holidays. Admission is free. In the same building is **The World of Puppets**, a display of over a hundred antique and contemporary puppets from around the world. Open weekdays 9 A.M. to 4 P.M.

Leidesdorff Street, a wide alley that runs between Clay and Pine streets just west of Sansome, used to be known as "Pauper Alley." Business was brisk in this part of town during the Gold Rush days. The alley was generally packed with messenger boys, brokers, and merchants who had business at the Pacific Stock Exchange or the San Francisco Mining Exchange. There was an assay office and a metallurgical works in a nearby basement. And, of course, the alley was crowded with restaurants and saloons—the Bonanza Saloon, the Red Rooster, and others. There was a special energy here; the atmosphere was spirited because the Comstock Mine in Virginia City was making millions of dollars from its flow of silver and gold. The smartly dressed men and women who walked these boardwalks could be rich one day and poor the next. Speculators crowded the alley waiting for prosperity to come on the announcement that a mining stock they had bought for pennies had turned out to be worth a

fortune. These hopefuls were called "mud hens," and they flocked to Leidesdorff Street like moths to a flame. Some lived in the open, begging for handouts while they waited for their lucky day to dawn.

The Bank of California, the first banking enterprise to open in the West, has its headquarters in a beautiful white granite building on the corner of California and Leidesdorff where it maintains the **Money of the American West Museum (256)**. Gold, that magical element, is displayed here—rare gold coins and nuggets as well as bars of the precious metal. Wall displays include paper money, rare Comstock Lode gold mining maps, historical artifacts, and old photographs. Each exhibit is accompanied by a well-researched text that history buffs will find of particular interest. The museum is in the basement safe deposit section of the bank. Open 10 A.M. to 2:30 P.M. weekdays only.

Near the corner of Leidesdorff Street at California, in front of the Wells Fargo Bank, is a relic from the past that might catch your eye—an old horse hitching post. Inside is a storage chamber that, in its day, held nosebags filled with oats or barley. The bags were to be draped around the heads of horses whose owners were patronizing the bank. This particular hitching post survived both the Comstock craziness of the 1860's and the earthquake and fire of 1906. It has also withstood the many changes that have occurred on this grand thoroughfare. The hitching post stands 5 feet tall on a 2-foot round base; four lion heads hold the rings for tying up reins.

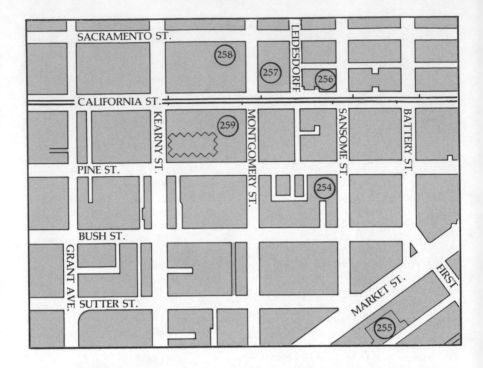

Montgomery Street

"Wall Street of the West"

Montgomery Street is named for the commander of the sloop-of-war *Portsmouth*, Captain John Berrian Montgomery. In 1846 Captain Montgomery claimed possession of the Mexican village of Yerba Buena, now San Francisco, in the name of the United States. The waterfront street that ran above the village high-water mark was named after this conquering American naval officer. Today Montgomery Street is the Wall Street of the West where you will find numerous large financial institutions and the office headquarters of many major corporations.

Wells Fargo Express started business in San Francisco in 1852 dispatching mail to the gold camps in the Sierra foothills. The formative years of this company offer a fascinating portrait of the Old West. **The Wells Fargo History Room (257)**, near the corner of Montgomery and California streets, is devoted to telling the story of the Wells Fargo Bank, a story set in the pioneering days of California. Here you'll find old paintings and photographs of the forty-niners, of famous characters such as Buffalo Bill, Black Bart, Bret Harte, and of the gold camps; gold nuggets, documents, tools, and equipment used by the early settlers; the desk at which Mark Twain wrote *Roughing It;* and much more. The center attraction in this excellent collection of artifacts is an authentic stagecoach used by the

company during its early days. For those interested in research, the Wells Fargo Bank has an extensive collection of books, photographs, manuscripts, and other research materials available for study. The curator in the history room will direct you to their library. Open 10 A.M. to 3 P.M. on regular banking days. Free admission.

The area around California and Montgomery streets was a popular promenade during San Francisco's early days. The city folks would come to stroll past the ships tied up with their long figure-headed bowsprits hanging over Montgomery Street. There was always a sidewalk show in the goings-on around the docks and all the colorful people passing by. One of those characters is still talked about today: Emperor Norton I—one of our town's folk heroes.

Joshua Abraham Norton was a successful rice merchant who hungered for riches. He tried to corner the rice market, but his gamble didn't pay off and instead forced him into bankruptcy. His loss drove him mad. He proclaimed himself "Norton I, Emperor of North America and Protector of Mexico." This is a town where eccentrics are indulged, and San Franciscans loved him. He wore the uniform of his fantasy, and every day he inspected his realm while riding his bicycle in the company of two dogs, Bummer and Lazarus. He levied taxes on other merchants, and they happily paid. The newspapers even published his proclamations. Emperor Norton died in 1880 on a Sunday afternoon while discussing the state of affairs with a group of churchgoers in front of Old St. Mary's Church, the red brick building on the corner of California Street and Grant Avenue.

San Francisco characters are legendary. Mark Twain and Robert Louis Stevenson wrote about many of them;

so did others. The list is long. Rudyard Kipling said, "San Francisco is a mad city—inhabited for the most part by perfectly insane people."

Jack's Restaurant (258), 615 Sacramento Street just west of Montgomery, is a San Francisco institution where the business community gathers and the dining room is always jammed. Jack's has been a meeting place for the City's social and political leaders since the mid-1860's. Several San Francisco personalities have regular tables reserved for them; if you want one held for you, be sure to phone ahead: 986-9854. Open Monday through Saturday from 11:30 A.M. to 9:15 P.M.; Sunday 5 P.M. to 9:15 P.M.

The world headquarters for the **Bank of America (259)** takes up the block between Montgomery and Kearny streets on California. The concourse level and the main floor feature a series of ongoing exhibits. The main lobby's massive walls make grand display areas for hanging contemporary paintings and tapestries. A second-level balcony area that looks down onto the main floor holds a permanent exhibit of antique business machines featuring early models of typewriters, calculators, and other office equipment. Open daily 10 A.M. to 4 P.M.

One of the most exhilarating skyscraper observation points that is accessible to the public is the **Carnelian Room** on the 52nd floor atop the Bank of America World Headquarters building, 555 California Street. This magnificent dining room and bar is *the* Financial District restaurant, and has been awarded numerous honors for its French and continental cuisine. Before 3 P.M. the Carnelian Room houses the Bankers' Club. Open to the public from 3 to 11:30 P.M.; on weekends from 4 P.M. till 1:30 A.M.. On Sunday, brunch begins at 10 A.M.

Grant Avenue

The heart of Chinatown

The California Street cable car line crosses Grant Avenue, the main thoroughfare of San Francisco's Chinatown. This is the City's oldest street. (See page 41 for a walking tour of Chinatown.)

The best vantage point as the cable car continues its steep climb up California Street is way at the back of the car. The view is spectacular, so get your camera ready.

Nob Hill

Powell Street to Jones Street

Nob Hill begins at the corner of Powell and California streets. There is always a crowd of visitors here, scurrying about with cameras. At this spot, the two cable car lines cross. The conductors do a lot of bell ringing, while a man in a tiny signal booth on the southeast corner controls the traffic signals and warns approaching cable cars of congestion.

During San Francisco's early days, Nob Hill, the loftiest peak in the City, was called "Hill of the Golden Promise." Nob is a slang expression derived from British sailors from "nabob," meaning a rich person. The main nobs of early San Francisco were a group of resolute men known to historians as the Big Four: Messrs. Crocker, Huntington, Hopkins, and Stanford. These gentlemen built a transcontinental railroad line, the Central Pacific Railroad, which became the Southern Pacific. During the 1860's and 1870's they, along with other rich and powerful men of the time, moved onto the hill and constructed palatial homes. All the homes had cavernous ballrooms where the Bonanza Kings and the railroad boys entertained on a grand scale. The ladies wore gowns of subdued elegance made either at the City of Paris or the White House, the two leading department stores of the City. Men wore swallow-tailed black jackets and white ties. Tables were laden with oysters, caviar, shrimp, salmon, duck, chicken, squab, ham, beef and venison, delicate pastries, and fine French wines, all ravishingly displayed under the glow of silver candelabras. It must have been a wonderful spectacle.

The small booth on the corner of Powell and California serves as an observation point from which cable car traffic is directed over the hill.

Nob Hill is crowned by a cluster of elegant hotels and a marvelous cathedral. The **Fairmont Hotel (260)**, at California and Mason, covers an entire city block on the eastern slope. It was built by the heirs of James G. Fair, "Bonanza Jim," one of the Irish lads who made the richest gold and silver strike in the world at the Comstock Mine in Virginia City, Nevada. The Fairmont is a beautiful white granite structure. Its steel frame survived the great 1906 earthquake and fire. In recent times, Fairmont owner Ben Swig added an apartment tower with an outside elevator that ascends 21 stories to an elegant roof-top restaurant and bar, the **Crown Room.** Needless to say, the view is breathtaking. Open Sunday through Thursday 11 A.M. to 1 A.M.; Friday and Saturday till 2 A.M.

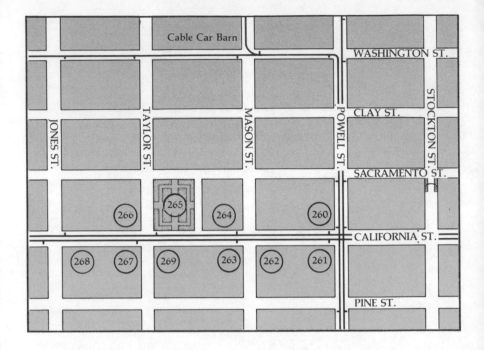

The Fairmont's sumptuous lobby preserves an old-world elegance that has all but faded from the American scene. The hotel has several fine restaurants and bars; there are gift shops and a small coffee shop on the main floor. Big name entertainment stars play the Fairmont's **Venetian Room** throughout the year; this room is also a popular dining and dancing spot. There is an entertainment charge, but no minimum. Open Tuesday through Sunday 7:30 P.M. to 1 A.M. Late nighters should try the **Brasserie** on the arcade floor; it's open around the clock for dinner and features Maine lobster.

Canlis' in the Fairmont Hotel is an elegant and sophisticated restaurant featuring a charcoal broiler in the center of a spacious dining room where chefs prepare gorgeous steaks, lobster, and chicken to your liking. Open daily 6 P.M. to midnight; cocktails from 5:30 P.M. to 2 A.M.. Reservations are advised: 392-0113.

The **Tonga Room,** also in the Fairmont, offers Chinese cuisine in a South Seas island atmosphere complete with a tropical storm on the half-hour that includes thunder, rain, and lightning. Cocktails and dancing Sunday to Thursday 5 P.M. to 1 A.M., Friday and Saturday 5 P.M. to 2 A.M.; dinner every day 6 P.M. to midnight. Reservations are advised: 772-5278.

The home of Leland Stanford used to stand at the corner of Powell and California streets, on the present site of the **Stanford Court Hotel (261).** Stanford, a man of great energy, was a partner in the building of the first transcontinental railroad, a governor of California, a United States senator, and founder of Stanford University in Palo Alto. The Stanford Court's solarium dining area, overlooking the cable car tracks, is a perfect place for breakfast or lunch. The hotel's pastry cook is a master French chef whose delectable creations will surely tempt you. Lunch daily 11:30 A.M. to 2:30 P.M.; dinner 5:30 to 11 P.M.

Overlooking the busy corner of California and Powell from the Stanford Court Hotel is a marvelous restaurant, **Fournou's Ovens.** The decor is French country focused around large open ovens heaped with hickory charcoal; above the fire prime rib, chicken and duckling, or a rack of lamb are roasted to your order. Open for lunch from 11:30 A.M. to 2 P.M., and dinner from 5:30 to 11 P.M. every day. Reservations are advised: 989-1910.

On an adjacent slope is another plush inn, the **Mark Hopkins Hotel (262).** At the turn of the century this choice property was the site of a huge Victorian home referred to by citizens of the City as "The Nob Hill Horror House." It was the home of Mark Hopkins, another partner in the building of the transcontinental railroad. When Hopkins died, the old house was left to the San Francisco Art Institute. After the earthquake and fire of 1906, the school moved to Russian Hill on Chestnut Street, and the hotel was constructed in its place. The **Top of the Mark** is a world-famous cocktail lounge with a view that is legendary. Open daily 10:30 A.M. to 2 A.M. The **Nob Hill Restaurant** offers superlative continental cookery including several flaming dishes which are served with great ceremony. Open every day for lunch from noon to 2:30 P.M., and for dinner from 6 P.M. to 11 P.M. Reservations are advised: 392-3434. The hotel has other restaurants and bars as well.

One of the City's more exotic restaurants is **Alexis (263),** at the corner of Mason and California streets. Owner Alexis Merab has named his bar the Casbah, and cocktail waitresses hover about in the dimly lit Middle East atmosphere. Anything you find on the menu is a taste treat, but we are partial to the rack of lamb and an hors d'oeuvre of blinis (crepes) stuffed with sour cream and caviar. Unforgettable. Open nightly except Sunday 6 P.M. till late.

James Flood, a saloon keeper who made millions investing in the Comstock gold and silver mine, built himself the stately mansion across California Street at the corner of Mason. This was the first and only brownstone building constructed in San Francisco. Today the building is the **Pacific Union Club (264),** clubhouse for a number of San Francisco's elite, known to many

A Huntington Park sculpture dedicated to the children of Nob Hill.

The magnificent Grace Cathedral and the stately brownstone Pacific Union Club crown the summit of Nob Hill.

as the "PU Club." The low fence that surrounds the building is solid bronze. In the past it was kept gleaming by a servant whose only job was to polish the fence daily.

Next door to the Pacific Union Club, in the shadow of the Mark Hopkins Hotel, is **Huntington Park (265)**, perhaps the most expensive piece of undeveloped land in the City. Fountains, benches, swings, and sandboxes make this quiet green space a favorite place for governesses and their charges.

Grace Cathedral (266), which faces the park on the west side, is well worth your inspection. Magnificent blue, gold and red stained-glass windows cast multicolored hues onto the Gothic interior. You'll be amazed at the variety and richness of the interior furnishings, which include bronze "Doors of Paradise" and an 11th century French high altar. Grace Cathedral is a diocesan church of the Episcopal Church of California. The church is open from 7 A.M. to 8 P.M.; tours are held daily between 3 P.M. and 4 P.M. A gift shop located in the plaza has a wide range of religious books, cards, and other attractive gifts. The shop hours are Monday through Saturday, 10 A.M. to 5 P.M.; Sunday, noon to 4 P.M.

That large white marble structure across California Street from Grace Cathedral is the **Masonic Memorial Auditorium (267)**. The auditorium acoustics makes this large hall an ideal location for lecture events and small musical productions.

If you plan a walking tour of this marvelous area of Nob Hill, begin with a breakfast at one of the two very good places close by. The **Vienna Coffee House** in the Mark Hopkins Hotel serves delicious pastries, fresh orange juice, and excellent coffees. Open from 7 A.M. to midnight. A second option is **Mama's (268)** at 1177 California Street near Jones. Mama's began as a small corner cafe in North Beach. The tasty fresh fruit and homemade breads and pastries proved to be a winning formula; there are now three Mama's restaurants around town. Open for breakfast and lunch Monday through Friday 8:30 A.M. to 3:30 P.M., and for dinner 5:30 P.M. to midnight (Friday until 1 A.M.). Open Saturday 9 A.M. to 1 A.M.; Sunday to 10 P.M.

A choice for brunch, lunch, or dinner might be the **Big Four Restaurant** in the **Huntington Hotel (269)** at 1075 California. This restaurant is named in memory of the railroad barons; the atmosphere is that of an Englishmen's private club. The food is continental, but the specialty is buffalo. The Huntington Hotel today is a virtual museum of Big Four memorabilia. These are posh places, so don't wear your Levis without your cowboy hat and gold chains, and have a credit card handy. Open 11:30 A.M. to 1 A.M.

L'Etoile at 1075 California Street is one of the City's more exclusive Nob Hill restaurants. Chef Claud Bougard is in full command and flies the essential ingredients for his menu offerings into San Francisco daily: lobster from Maine, veal from Canada, scallops from Cape Cod, and strawberries from France. The atmosphere in this award-winning spot is Parisian plush. Open 6 P.M. to 10:30 P.M.; closed Sunday. Reservations are advised: 771-1529. The exceptionally entertaining pianist Peter Mintun plays nostalgic tunes in the bar Tuesday through Saturday from 8:30 until closing.

A California Street cable car rumbles across Polk Street on its way downtown.

Polk Street and Van Ness Avenue

The end of the line

When the cable car rattles to a stop at the bottom of the hill at Polk Street, almost everyone gets off. The end of the line is only one block farther at Van Ness Avenue, San Francisco's auto row. This last cable car stop is also the location of the **Van Ness Avenue Holiday Inn (270)**.

This part of Polk Street is populated largely by the City's gay community. (A second popular gay neighborhood is an area on Castro Street near Market at the foot of Twin Peaks.) Traditionally this neighborhood has been a residential business district, but the growing gay population has caused an influx of tourists, coffee houses, bars, boutiques, and discos. You'll find a lot to explore on Polk Street; we'll mention just a few of the places you may want to visit.

Two movie theaters serve the neighborhood—the **Royal (271)** at 1529 Polk Street and the **Lumiere (272)** at 1572 California, around the corner.

Paperback Traffic (273) is a large and very well stocked bookstore on the corner of California and Polk streets. Neighborhood book shops tend to be short on variety, but that is not the case here. You'll find a lot of general interest books as well as an excellent selection of large format gift books on theater, the arts, and ballet. Open 10 A.M. to 10 P.M. every day.

When it's time to have lunch, try **Swan's Oyster Depot (274)**, a small but excellent seafood cafe at 1517 Polk. This small restaurant is operated by Sal Sancimino and his six sons. It is a fish market with a cold bar. The only hot food served is chowder. Mr. Sancimino's father started the shop in 1912, selling fresh fish and serving hot chowders with crab and shrimp salads. In the intervening years nothing has changed. All the fixtures are the originals—the wire counter stools, the mirrors, the marble counters, the white-tiled walls and floors. It's old San Francisco alive and well on Polk Street. Moderately expensive. Open daily 10 A.M. to 5 P.M.

Polk Street south of the cable car track is populated by a number of small antique shops and auction houses as well as boutiques and several small restaurants. At 1411 Polk Street is a good pizzeria. **Victor's (275)**, is a small informal cafe with a counter; the pizza seems to more than satisfy the crowds that pack the place. Open 11:30 A.M. to late.

The Palms (276) at 1406 Polk was one of the City's first rock'n'roll clubs. They recently began their second decade providing a venue for stars of the rock world. There is an entertainment cover charge of $2 to $4 depending on the program. No food. Open 1 P.M. to 2 A.M. Tuesday to Sunday, Monday 3 P.M. to 2 A.M.

A few steps farther, is a bit of old San Francisco that attracts visitors from long distances and is very popular with City residents—**Freed Teller & Freed (277)**, 1326 Polk. The same family clan has been offering imported teas, coffees, fine jams and jellies, and

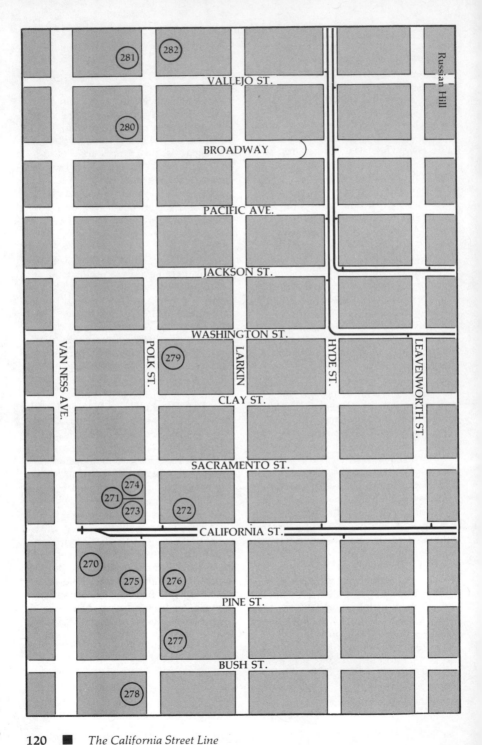

coffee-making equipment at this location for four generations. The original cherry wood and glass coffee bins and 1890's store fixtures haven't been changed in nearly a century of use. This is one of the few shops in town that somehow escaped the devastating earthquake and fire of 1906. It's worth a visit. Open 9:30 A.M. to 5:30 P.M.; closed Sunday.

La Piazza (278), 1247 Polk, is a pizza shop that is as much a social gathering place as it is a good restaurant. The food brings together a fascinating mix of people. Open 11 A.M. to 11 P.M.

If you walk north along Polk you will come to the neighborhood's shopping district—drug stores, ice cream parlors, record shops, boutiques, restaurants, and specialty shops. Also along Polk Street are a number of small shops offering antiques and collectibles.

We found a modestly priced French restaurant, **Le Tournesol (279)**, at 1760 Polk. It offers an intimate dining atmosphere with baskets of flowers and hanging copper pots for decoration. The specialty of the house is fresh filet of salmon with mousseline of lobster and scallops baked in puff pastry. The filet of roast lamb also looks very good. Open daily for lunch from 11:30 A.M. to 2:30 P.M.; dinner is served from 5 to 11:30 P.M. Reservations are advised: 441-1760.

The next few blocks, between Clay Street and Broadway, are chockfull of places to shop and browse. The stores all have a look of individuality that characterizes this part of San Francisco. If you want a quick bite to eat as you walk along, there are many choices: stop for a slice of pizza, an ice cream cone, or an outstanding hot dog from the Noble Frankfurter.

If you are fond of cut-glass mirrors, Tiffany lamps, stained glass and Victorian furniture, you'll enjoy relaxing over a cocktail at **Lord Jim's (280)**, on the corner of Broadway and Polk. This is a popular watering hole for young singles. A party atmosphere prevails, and you'll find a lot of lovely people to ogle. Open 11:30 A.M. till late.

Xenios (281) is an interesting Greek restaurant at 2237 Polk Street. It specializes in lamb dishes, dolmades, and moussaka. A thoroughly Greek atmosphere. Open every day 11 A.M. to 11 P.M.

The **Alhambra Theatre (282)** is typical of the large ornate movie houses of the 1930's found in San Francisco. Around it is yet another clutch of small restaurants and coffee houses.

Polk Street continues out to Aquatic Park. It's a long walk, but you can catch a #19 bus headed north anywhere along Polk Street. Or you can retrace your route on the California Street cable car and return to any of the places that especially appealed to you.

Riding the cable cars and exploring the City is a continuing adventure for San Franciscans, and an all-too-short adventure for visitors. Romance and adventure await you everywhere in this marvelous town. We've shared our favorite places—places that we know from experience or reputation—but there is much more. The City by the Golden Gate has been the dream at the end of the rainbow, the prize and the goal for countless pioneers. There is magic here, and we know that you'll find it.

TRANSPORTATION TO
OTHER POINTS OF INTEREST

When you pay your fare (50¢) on either a cable car or any other form of MUNI transportation, ask for a transfer. It will allow you to change to other buses or cable cars going in the same general direction for up to two hours. Below we have listed some of the most popular attractions that are not within easy walking distance of the cable car lines but which can be easily reached by transferring to other MUNI lines. Most any bus ride turns into a scenic tour of the City, and most bus drivers are happy to call out your stop for you—just ask as you board the bus.

Civic Center, including City Hall, the Opera House, Davies Symphony Hall, and the Museum of Modern Art: take the #5 westbound on Market Street to Van Ness Avenue.

Cliff House, Seal Rock, and Ocean Beach: take the #38 on Geary Street to 48th Avenue and Point Lobos, then walk down the hill.

Exploratorium, the Palace of Fine Arts, Marina Green, and Yacht Harbor: take the #30 bus from the southeast corner of Third and Market streets to the end of the line at Broderick and Beach streets. Walk one block west.

Fort Mason Center and the Youth Hostel: take the #30 bus from the southeast corner of Third and Market streets to Chestnut and Laguna streets. Walk north along Laguna toward the Bay, which is several blocks away.

Golden Gate Bridge and Fort Point: take a Golden Gate Transit bus from Market and Seventh streets north to the Toll Plaza. Or you can take the #30 bus from Third and Market streets to Chestnut and Fillmore. Transfer to the #28 bus which also goes to the Golden Gate Bridge Toll Plaza.

Golden Gate Park (the M. H. de Young Museum and the Asian Art Museum, the California Academy of Sciences Museum, including the Morrison Planetarium and Steinhart Aquarium, and the Japanese Tea Garden): take the #5 bus on Market Street to Fulton Street at 8th Avenue. From here you can walk into the park or transfer to the #44 which stops in front of the museums and Tea Garden, then continues through the park to the Hall of Flowers and Strybing Arboretum. On its return through the park, the #44 stops on the opposite side of the Music Concourse, in front of the Steinhart Aquarium and the Science Museum. If you would rather not wait for a #44 bus, you can walk into the park to the museums; it's only a short five-block walk. Also, roller skates and bicycles can be rented along this section of Fulton Street.

Golden Gate Park's magnificent Conservatory of Flowers and Plants is close to the M. H. de Young Museum, the Aquarium, and Natural History Museum.

To visit the **Conservatory of Flowers,** you can take either the #5 or #21 bus to Stanyan Street. Walk down the hill to Kennedy Drive and turn right. The ivy-covered building near the corner is McLaren Lodge, the park headquarters. There you can get an excellent map of the park. Continue along Kennedy Drive to the Conservatory. From there you can continue west to the places mentioned above.

Japantown: take the #38 Geary Street bus to Laguna Street. Or you can take the #1, #2, #3, or #4 bus westbound on Sutter Street to Buchanan Street.

Mission Dolores: on Market Street take the J streetcar westbound to 16th and Church, walk one block east to Dolores Street.

Union Square Shopping District: take the #45 bus on Sutter Street and get off anywhere between Gough and Steiner streets.

Zoo: take the L Muni Metro from any of the Market Street stations. The Muni Metro runs underneath Market Street; you enter at the BART stations.

More detailed information is available from the following sources:

MUNI (all local transportation)—673-6864
AC Transit (East Bay buses)—654-7878
BART (East Bay and Daly City trains)—788-2278
Golden Gate Transit (Marin and Sonoma buses)—332-6600
Greyhound—433-1500
SamTrans (Airport and Peninsula buses)—761-7000
Trailways—982-6400
Ferry information:
    Alcatraz—546-2805
    Angel Island—546-2815
    Sausalito and Larkspur—982-8834
    Tiburon—546-2815

GLOSSARY

AMUSEMENTS

Chinatown Wax Museum, 43
Enchanted World of Old San Francisco, 76
Haunted Gold Mine, 76
Pier 39 Arcade and Merry-Go-Round, 79
Ripley's Believe It Or Not, 76
San Francisco Experience, 25
Wax Museum 76

ANTIQUES AND COLLECTIBLES

Paul's Antiques, 38
Sergio Old Prints, 22
Shlock Shop, 89
Stewart's Treasure House, 36

ART GALLERIES

Contemporary Artisans, 41
Cory Gallery, 25
Gallery One, 35
John Pence Gallery, 35
Light Opera, 64
Pasquale Iannette Gallery, 35
Stephen Wirtz Gallery, 32
Swanson Gallery, 35

ART SUPPLIES

Flax Art Supply, 39
Michael's Artist Supplies, 38

BOOK STORES

Albert Henry Books, 27
B. Dalton Bookseller, 39
Brentano's, 39
City Lights, 96
Cookbook Corner, 37
Drama Book Shop, 27
Harold's (out-of-town newspapers), 26
International Corner, 35
John Howell Books, 28
Paperback Traffic, 119
Sierra Club Bookstore, 41
Tillman Place Bookshop, 30
Tro Harper's Book Store, 14
Waldenbooks, 19

BOUTIQUES

Andre Courrege, 22
Barra of Italy, 69
East/West Leather, 89
Gucci, 30
Helga Howie, 22
Kyriakos of Hydra, 89
Mistress, The, 69
North Beach Leathers, 69
Obiko, 36
Rupp & Taureck, 32
Tannery, The, 69
White Duck Workshop, 35
Wilkes Bashford, 38

CHURCHES AND TEMPLES

Grace Cathedral, 116
Kong Chow Temple, 45
Kwan Yin Temple, 45
Old St. Mary's, 44
Our Lady of Guadalupe, 94
St. Peter and Paul s Church, 85
Tien Hau Temple, 45

DELICATESSENS AND BAKERIES

Boudin French Bread Shop, 72
David's Delicatessen, 27
Just Desserts, 54
Mee Mee Bakery, 50
Molinari's, 92
Panelli Brothers, 92
Stage Delicatessen, 26
Victoria Pastry Co., 82

DEPARTMENT STORES

Brooks Brothers, 30
Bullock & Jones, 29
Emporium, 12–13
Gumps, 30
Hastings, 33
I. Magnin, 18
Joseph Magnin, 18
Liberty House, 18
Livingston's, 33
Macy's, 18
Saks Fifth Avenue, 28

FABRICS

Britex Fabrics, 19
Pierre Deux Original Fabrics, 35

GIFT AND SPECIALTY SHOPS

A. Dunhill of London, 29
Bath, The, 69
Candy Jar, 32
Captain's Wharf, 14
City of Hankow Tassel Co., 42
City of Shanghai, 43
Come Fly a Kite, 64
Cost Plus, 74
Freed, Teller & Freed, 119
Gucci, 30
Indian Trading Post, 42
Irish Castle, 27
Jacqueline St. Francis Perfume Shop, 24
Jim Mate Pipe Shop, 27
Johnson & Joseph Chandlery, 68
La Ville du Soleil, 36
Light Opera, 64

Malm Luggage, 32
Morrow's Nut Shop, 19
Podesta Baldocci, 31
Postermart, 92
Scotch House, 32
Scottish Tartan Shop, 27
Wedgewood China Ltd., 29

HOME FURNISHINGS

Mobilia, 33
W & J Sloan, 39

JEWELERS

Granat Brothers, 20
Nina's Pearls and Jade, 25
Pearl Empire, 19
Shreve & Co., 30
Sidney Mobell, 32
Theodora, 21
Tiffany & Co., 31
Vince's Jewelry, 25
Whitehall Company, 19

KITCHENWARE

Caravansary, 38
Exclusive Cutlery Shop, 18
Figoni Hardware, 89
John Simmons Store, 36
Williams-Sonoma Kitchenware, 36

MUSEUMS AND EXHIBITS

Balclutha, 67
Cable Car Barn and Museum, 51
Chinatown Wax Museum, 43
Chinese Culture Center, 47
Geology Museum, 101
Hyde Street Pier, 67
Maritime Museum, 65
Money Museum of the American West, 107
Museo Italo Americano, 88
North Beach Museum, 93
Old Mint, 11
Pacific Stock Exchange, 106
Ripley's Believe It Or Not, 76
Wax Museum, 76
Wells Fargo History Room, 108
Wine Museum, 69
World of Oil, 107
World of Puppets, 107

NIGHT LIFE

PARKS

PHOTO SUPPLIES

RESTAURANTS AND BARS

Portofino Caffe, 64
Powell Street Bar and Grill, 83
Rosebud's English Grill, 25
Sabella's, 72
Salmugundi, 27
Schroeder's, 104
Scoma's, 72
Sears Restaurant, 33
Stage Delicatessen, 27
Swan's Oyster Depot, 119
Tadich Grill, 104
Tarantino's, 72
Templebar, 31
Tonga Room, 114
Top of the Mark, 115
Trader Vic's, 29
Vanessi's, 97
Veneto's, 74
Vesuvio Cafe, 96
Via Veneto, 64
Victor's, 119
Washington Square Bar and Grill, 83
Xenios, 121
Yamato Sukiyaki House, 43

SHOPPING AREAS

Anchorage, 71
Cannery, 68
Embarcadero Center, 102
Geary Street, 17
Ghirardelli Square, 64
Grant Avenue, 30
Maiden Lane, 21
Pier 39, 78
Post Street, 28
Sutter Street, 35
Union Square, 17

SPORTING GOODS

Don Sherwood's Golf and Tennis World, 31
Eddie Bauer, 30
Johnson & Joseph Chandlery, 68
Mountain Shop, 32
Orvis, 22
Tennis Lady, 22

THEATERS

Alhambra Theatre, 121
American Conservatory Theatre, 26
Curran Theatre, 26
Lumiere Theatre, 119
Masonic Memorial Auditorium, 117
Royal Theatre, 119
San Francisco Experience, 25
Sun Sing Theater, 50

TOURS AND FERRIES

Alcatraz Island, 78
Angel Island, 77
Bay Cruises, 76
Blue & Gold Fleet, 76
Commodore Helicopters, 77
Dashiell Hammett, 54
Ferries to Tiburon, Sausalito, and Larkspur,
    101
Gold Coast Cruise, 76
Gray Line, 17
Sail Tours, 77

TOYS

F. A. O. Schwarz, 32
Hobby Co., 38
Jeffrey's Toys, 38

VIEW POINTS

Carnelian Room, 110
Coit Tower, 87
Crookedest Street, 57
Crown Room, 112
Equinox, 102
Henri's Room at the Top, 13
Russian Hill Park, 57
Russian Hill summit, 55
Starlite Roof, 33
Top of the Mark, 115
Transamerica Pyramid, 95
Victor's, 24

VISITOR SERVICES

American Express, 30
Convention and Visitors Bureau, 10
Redwood Empire Visitors Center, 29

INDEX